WE
FOLLOW
CHRIST

edited by Tara Beth Leach,
Patricia M. Batten, and Matthew D. Kim

WE

FOLLOW

CHRIST

Helping Women to Discern God's Call

Foreword by Linda A. Livingstone
Afterword by Nijay K. Gupta

1845BOOKS

Cover and book design by Elyxandra Encarnación
Cover image: Pexels/Rodolfo Quirós

Library of Congress Cataloging-in-Publication Data

Names: Leach, Tara Beth, 1982– editor. | Batten, Patricia M., editor. | Kim, Matthew D., 1977– editor.

Title: We follow Christ: helping women to discern God's call / Tara Beth Leach, Patricia M. Batten, and Matthew D. Kim, editors; foreword by Linda A. Livingstone; afterword by Nijay K. Gupta.

Description: Waco, Texas: Baylor University Press, [2025] | Summary: "Women called to different roles in ministry discuss the joys and challenges of Christian vocation"—Provided by publisher.

Identifiers: LCCN 2024056198 (print) | LCCN 2024056199 (ebook) | ISBN 9781481322805 (paperback) | ISBN 9781481322829 (adobe pdf) | ISBN 9781481322812 (epub)

Subjects: LCSH: Women in church work. | Women in Christianity. | Vocation—Christianity.

Classification: LCC BV4415.W34 2025 (print) | LCC BV4415 (ebook) | DDC 253.082—dc23/eng/20250723

LC record available at https://lccn.loc.gov/2024056198
LC ebook record available at https://lccn.loc.gov/2024056199

To women of every stage of life who seek to follow
God's calling in their lives.

CONTENTS

I

Finding Your Calling

II

Calling in Church Ministry

III

Calling in Other Ministries

IV

Calling in Academic Ministry

FOREWORD

Linda A. Livingstone

Linda A. Livingstone is the fifteenth president of Baylor University. A native of Perkins, Oklahoma, Dr. Livingstone played varsity basketball at Oklahoma State University. Her husband, Brad, a high school history teacher, also played basketball at Oklahoma State. They have one daughter, Shelby, who also contributed to this volume.

When I look back over my journey, several themes emerge. The first is the importance of embracing your passions as a pathway to leadership. In my case, the passion that eventually led me to pursue advanced degrees and work in higher education came in many ways from the life of my parents, who had a unique influence on me.

My story begins on the plains of rural Oklahoma. My father, Doyle, played basketball at Oklahoma A&M University (now Oklahoma State) and in the NBA, and he eventually became a college basketball coach in Oklahoma. He came from a small farm in southwestern Oklahoma, where he grew up picking cotton. As the first person in his family to go to college, my father single-handedly established a legacy of higher education that now extends two generations and will be multiplied for many generations to come. From my father, I gained a competitive spirit and a love of athletics early in life. I grew up playing basketball in Gallagher Hall at Oklahoma State after his practices ended. Through these shared experiences playing sports, my father instilled in me the belief that I could accomplish whatever I set my mind to, if I worked at it and dedicated myself to it.

My mother, Charlotte, was a kindergarten and second-grade schoolteacher. She is a true servant at heart. She delivered Meals on Wheels until she was almost eighty-five! And at ninety-four, she still volunteers at her church every day and is on the local library board. From her, I gained the desire to make a difference in the lives of others, no matter what I was doing. This dedication to service, combined with my competitive nature, nurtured through athletics, led me to leadership roles at an early age.

In college, I followed in my father's footsteps by playing basketball for Oklahoma State University. I also became involved in the Fellowship of Christian Athletes. Like many undergraduates, I was often undecided about my future profession, but I knew that I wanted to do something that would combine my love of athletics, my desire to make a difference, and my Christian faith.

As I considered my professional options, I had a personal encounter during my first year that proved to be life-altering. My now-husband, Brad, received an article in OSU's magazine from his father with my picture circled. Brad's father, who did not know me at all, told him, "This is the kind of young woman you should be dating." When Brad shared this with me in the hallway between classes our first year, we both laughed it off, but then I started running into Brad at basketball practices and Fellowship of Christian Athletes meetings. We started dating in my junior year. In September of 1983, on a day that coincided with an OSU football game, Brad and I were married. True to form, Brad and his groomsmen watched the game while getting ready for the wedding, and they cheered so loudly everyone in the church could hear them. Incidentally, the OSU Cowboys beat the Texas A&M Aggies by a score of 34–15 that day. It was clearly a good start to a long and happy marriage!

I will be forever grateful that Brad's father sent him that copy of OSU's magazine, even though it produced one of the worst pickup lines I have ever heard! Brad is a true partner with me on life's journey and my best friend.

Toward the end of my undergraduate experience, I began to look at graduate school. I was fortunate enough to finish my undergraduate work one semester early and still had a semester of athletic eligibility and a semester of school paid for, so I began my MBA. There was not a particularly strategic reason to go to graduate school, but it was practical then. During that program, one of my professors, Dr. John Mowen, asked me if I had ever considered getting a PhD. At that point, I had not, but that one comment planted a seed that stuck with me over the next few years, eventually motivating me to go back to Oklahoma State University to earn a doctorate in business administration.

I loved working on my PhD. I was exhilarated by the prospect of spending a career facilitating people's learning and knew I'd finally found my professional calling. Now, I just had to get hired!

My doctoral advisor at Oklahoma State was a woman named Dr. Debra Nelson. During my time in graduate school, I spent many hours in Dr. Nelson's office discussing my dissertation and the job market for budding academics. Dr. Nelson knew that my faith was a fundamental part of my life, and one day, she asked me, "Have you ever thought about applying to teach at a Baptist school in Texas called Baylor University?"

At the time, I hadn't considered applying to Baylor. I didn't know anyone who had attended Baylor—Oklahoma State and Baylor were in different conferences at the time, and I had never been on the Baylor campus. But, on Dr. Nelson's recommendation, I reached out to the university.

Sure enough, it just so happened that the year I applied to Baylor, the business school had an opening in my field! I applied for the position and got the job. We moved to Waco in 1991. Baylor was a perfect fit. The Christian environment was stimulating, the academic environment was challenging, and I was able to continue my involvement in athletics via the Faculty Athletics Council.

In fact, my opportunity to serve on the Faculty Athletics Council came in part because of my skills as a basketball player. And this also relates to a second major theme in my journey, which is to take advantage of seemingly insignificant opportunities, because sometimes the smallest events turn out to have the largest impact on your future.

In my second or third year at Baylor, the university hosted a faculty free-throw shooting contest to launch the new basketball season. As I arrived that night and lined up along the baseline for the competition, I looked down the baseline and noticed I was the only woman along with twenty or so male faculty members in the competition. Brad was in the stands and overheard some fans commenting, "Why in the world did they allow a girl in the competition?" As luck (and maybe a little talent) would have it, I won that free-throw shooting contest. The next year I happened to win the contest again, and for some reason they canceled the competition for future years! It was amazing how much visibility on campus winning that first competition gave me and how many opportunities I then had for involvement and leadership, including serving on the Faculty Athletics Council. I learned from this experience to pay attention to insignificant events, as these can turn out to be important transition moments in your life.

Shortly after I received tenure at Baylor, the chair of my department, Dr. Don Edwards, asked me, "Have you ever thought about transitioning from a full-time faculty role into administration?" Shortly thereafter, I was asked to serve as Associate Dean for Graduate Programs in the Business School, launching my career into university administration.

By now, I'm sure you've noticed a third theme in my leadership journey—listening to people who know you well. Without Dr. Mowen encouraging me to pursue my PhD, Dr. Nelson encouraging me to apply for a position at Baylor, and Dr. Edwards encouraging me to enter administration, I never would have ended up where I am today.

Around the time I began serving as an associate dean at Baylor's business school, my daughter, Shelby, was born. My first eleven years at Baylor had been happy and formative, and my husband and I had no intentions of leaving Waco.

But a colleague of mine, Dr. Blaine McCormick, nominated me for the dean's position at Pepperdine University's Graziadio School of Business and Management. This nomination was unexpected, and Brad and I knew it would be a major change for our family. In fact, Brad's initial reaction was, "Why would we want to leave Baylor? Where is Pepperdine anyway?" When I told him Malibu, California, he said, "Well, we should at least go check it out." As Brad describes it, we then "bathed this decision in prayer," and ultimately felt God leading us to Pepperdine. (Word of advice here—if you are ever "called" to Malibu, California, just know that people take that calling with a grain of salt . . . or a grain of sand.)

At Pepperdine, I walked into a challenging situation where the previous dean had been removed and distrust pervaded the culture among faculty and staff. Despite the obstacles, I was happy and fulfilled during my time at Pepperdine. But after years, I started to wonder about the next steps in my journey. Others had reached out to me to consider opportunities as a dean, a provost, and even a president. I began to sense that the leadership skills I was honing as a dean might one day lead me to yet a higher level of administrative service. But I had no idea what that might be.

In 2014, I took another crucial step in my journey by going to George Washington University in Washington, D.C. to serve as the dean of the school of business. Once again, I walked into a challenging situation where the dean had been removed unceremoniously and dissension and angst pervaded the faculty and staff. In retrospect, I've realized how formative my combined experiences at Pepperdine and GW were to my development as a leader. I went into challenging situations at both institutions, and sometimes I wondered if I had made the right choice. Brad always had faith, however, and many times told me that God was preparing me for something even more significant.

That something occurred in 2017 when I received the call informing me that I had been selected as the fifteenth president of Baylor University. I felt that, once again, God was asking me to take a leap of faith. At that time, Baylor had made national headlines due to an institutional failure to respond appropriately to reports of sexual assault, especially those involving students on our football team. The scandal led to the ousting of the president and football coach at the time, as well as the resignation of the athletic director.

Even from a distance, I was fully aware of the pain that the Baylor family was experiencing. I also understood that we would continue to deal with ongoing investigations about these issues for the next several years. As with every other move we had made up to that point, Brad, Shelby, and I understood that accepting this position would be a major change for our family.

So we once again bathed this decision in prayer. It soon became evident to all of us that God was bringing us back to Baylor. I was excited by the opportunity not only to return to a university that I loved, but to a place I felt God had been preparing me to lead. I accepted the call not despite recent institutional difficulties but because of them. Every crisis is an opportunity to learn and rebuild, and God wanted me to assume this task at this point in Baylor's history. I decided early in my career that I didn't want to be the type of person who says, "This is all there is," but that I wanted to stay ready for new challenges and new opportunities to serve, even if that ended up leading me down a difficult path.

It has now been seven years since I answered the call to serve as the president of Baylor. And those seven years have held some tremendous accomplishments and some of my favorite memories. Through the dedication and hard work of our faculty and staff, the Carnegie Classification of Institutions of Higher Education classified Baylor as a Research 1 institution. We raised over $1.5 billion in our most successful philanthropic campaign in institutional history. Both our men's and women's basketball teams won national championships. And we are continuing to move towards our goal of becoming America's preeminent Christian research university.

My last seven years at Baylor have certainly come with their challenges, too. We had to restore trust in our faculty and staff and in a shaken alumni base. We navigated the pandemic. We have faced our share of detractors and naysayers. But God had prepared me for such a time as this.

As I reflect on my sense of calling and the purpose of this book, I will share one more formative experience in my calling journey—maybe one of the most formative. It occurred while I was a professor at Baylor in the 1990s. I was the vice-chair of the pastor search committee for Calvary Baptist Church in Waco, Texas. Through the leading of the Holy Spirit, the committee recommended that a woman be called to lead the church. She would be the first woman pastor of a Baptist congregation in Texas. As you can imagine, the pushback was swift. As the church became embroiled in a hotbed of unwanted controversy, both strangers and close friends lambasted those of us on the search committee. But we were confident that calling this senior pastor was clearly God's work. And we did not cave to the demands of our critics. In 1998, Reverend Julie Pennington-Russell became the first woman to serve as senior pastor of a Baptist congregation in Texas. She remains a close friend to this day.

Through this experience I gained a tremendous amount of self-knowledge, a better understanding of the importance of standing by my convictions, and an ability to deal with criticism from close friends. These are all skills that I've relied heavily upon in the twenty-five years since her hiring, especially as Baylor's president. The moments of greatest rejection have produced in me the resilience I have needed to lead effectively.

I want to leave you with an exhortation from Hebrews 10. The author is speaking to persecuted Jewish Christians in the early church who had experienced different hardships in their faith journeys. In verses 35–36, the author writes, "So do not throw away your confidence; it will be richly rewarded. You need to persevere so that when you have done the will of God, you will receive what he has promised" (NIV).

My encouragement to women exploring their calling is this: don't throw away your confidence. It will be richly rewarded.

This spring, I attended a screening of the documentary *Midwives of a Movement*, produced by Baptist Women in Ministry. The film honors the God-ordained callings of Baptist women over decades, and it acknowledges the many obstacles these women faced in pursuit of their callings. Several of the women interviewed in the film were at the screening, and many in the room have been role models for younger female ministry leaders, including my daughter, Shelby, who was ordained nearly two years ago. It was powerful to be in the same room with them and to celebrate how their obedience and courage have blazed trails for future women to lead, minister, and fulfill God's call for their lives.

These women didn't throw away their confidence. And their perseverance is being richly rewarded as they pass the baton of ministry to the next generation of women leaders.

Just as women before you persevered and responded to God's call for their lives, settle for nothing less. Your confidence and perseverance will be richly rewarded.

I am proud of the hard work, advocacy, and affirmation of women in ministry, leadership, and every field God calls us to. And I look forward to seeing how God will use this next generation of leaders to change the world for his glory.

ACKNOWLEDGMENTS

We are blessed to be supported by Baylor University's president, Linda A. Livingstone, in this project. As you will discover from reading her splendid foreword, she is a remarkable Christian leader and person. Thank you, President Livingstone, for championing Christ, the church, the scriptures, Baylor University, and beyond, including the ministry of women.

We are grateful to Dave Nelson, director of Baylor University Press, for his enthusiastic support to publish this book. Thanks to the entire team at 1845 Books who guided this work from start to finish.

Thanks to all our wonderful contributors who work in such diverse fields for the glory of God. We appreciate the profound wisdom you've shared in these pages giving insight into how you've navigated your calling into these respective areas of influence. Many thanks to Nijay K. Gupta for crafting a perceptive and hopeful afterword.

Lastly, deepest appreciation goes out to our great and glorious triune God: Father, Son, and Holy Spirit, who gifts and calls women and men for kingdom work and impact. All glory to God!

INTRODUCTION

Matthew D. Kim

Matthew D. Kim is Professor of Preaching and Pastoral Leadership, holder of the George W. Truett Endowed Chair in Preaching and Evangelism, and Director of the PhD in Preaching program at George W. Truett Theological Seminary, Baylor University, Waco, Texas.

As I sat in an evening worship gathering on a college campus, the preacher was being introduced. A woman walked up the steps and stood at the podium. Immediately, I saw a man sitting near the front of the auditorium get up and excuse himself at that very moment. As he turned to the side, I recognized him. Knowing him to be a complementarian with regard to women in ministry, I understood that he frowned on female preachers.

Yet it's one thing to hold to a particular view and check out mentally. Witnessing him physically protest with his feet, however, was disappointing. The severity of his ministry ideology which led to vacating the worship space of God was a waving of the banner of sorts: "I don't support female preachers!" Was there absolutely nothing he could learn from her message?

This book is a clarion call to say that in all things, we (women *and* men) follow Christ and pursue the callings that God alone invites us to. We don't follow people's rules or human prohibitions. We go where Jesus sends and serve how he instructs.

If women were prohibited from participating in all parts of kingdom work, why would God equip women with so many gifts and talents in those roles? If you are feeling resistant, agitated, or angry about what you've just read, please ask yourself some honest questions: Why do I feel this way? Whose perspective did I learn about this topic? What did they say? How did I come to my own view? And, for some, what do I need to know to decide?

The enemy, Satan, and his little sidekicks divide and conquer wherever and whenever opportunity strikes. What better for the kingdom of darkness than to create and continue rifts between men and women, women versus women, and men versus men? Satan devours people, especially Christians, willing to split the church. He applauds, celebrates, and dances when Christ followers despise, gossip, humiliate, mock, ridicule, and slander others publicly and privately "in the name of Jesus" and "for the sake of the church."

Sometimes the best advocate for another person or group is not a member of that demographic but someone from the outside—in this instance, a man speaking up for women. The genesis of this book is that as a male professor, pastor, and author, I believe I can make a difference. Why?

While in society I am an ethnic minority, in terms of gender I have an advantage simply by being a man. I wasn't forced to choose between having a career and having a family. Nobody contested my participation in any church or academic office. Nobody questioned or challenged my calling to ordained ministry and later my pursuit of theological education. Therefore, I am entering the conversation to be "a voice for the voiceless" and standing with and for women. Not that women don't already have voices, for they surely do. They are moms, community leaders, pastors of churches, professors, authors, counselors, leaders of universities and organizations, CEOs of successful companies, surgeons and doctors, Supreme Court justices, presidents of nations, and more.

But I believe we can do better, and in many cases, much better, particularly in Christian circles. While I am not blessed to have daughters myself, I am hoping that in this next generation families with daughters will have no need for books like this. It will be assumed that women can do all the things that men can do. This book is a first-of-its-kind resource to guide women in discerning and living God's call.

The unique and gifted contributors to this volume are leaders in their respective fields in the church, in theological education, and in society. I've tapped their shoulders to share collective wisdom and experiences in being called by God and exercising that call. Reflecting on their journeys, they disclose transparent stories of heartache and yet offer hope in the one whom they have chosen to follow, the Lord Jesus Christ.

I am also delighted that dear colleagues and friends have joined me to serve as editors:

First, Tara Beth Leach is the senior pastor of Good Shepherd Church in Naperville, Illinois. She is a gifted pastor, preacher, teacher, and author. She has written bestselling books, including *Emboldened: A Vision for Empowering Women in Ministry* and *Radiant Church: Restoring the Credibility of Our Witness*, in addition to several other publications. She has been an exemplary pastoral shepherd for over two decades.

Second, Patricia M. Batten, a professor of preaching and associate director of the Haddon W. Robinson Center for Preaching at Gordon-Conwell Theological Seminary in South Hamilton, Massachusetts, is a seasoned and skilled senior pastor, preacher, and teacher. She's the author of *Parenting by Faith: What Jesus Said to Parents* and coeditor with the late Haddon W. Robinson of *Models for Biblical Preaching: Expository Sermons from the Old Testament*. Her PhD from the University of Aberdeen, under Professor John Swinton, explored the intersection of preaching and intellectual disability.

As you read these contributions of women serving Christ, remember that God alone calls and equips. There is no wrong way to follow the call of Christ because all of life is an opportunity for ministry service. There is no "less than" or "greater than" calling for any person. We are all ministers of the gospel with different expressions.

The four parts of this book provide different areas of work to consider. Taking a posture of openness, invite God to show you his plan, which you may not have explored. My hope in serving as an editor is to promote and champion you: Pursue your dreams to the glory of God. Be encouraged, empowered, and free! And most importantly, follow Christ!

Let's start this road to freedom by learning what it means to be called and how to discern God's calling.

I
Finding Your Calling

1
FINDING YOUR CALLING

Angie Ward

Angie Ward is Director of the Doctor of Ministry and Associate Professor of Leadership and Ministry at Denver Seminary. Her books include *I Am a Leader: When Women Discover the Joy of Their Calling* and *Uncharted Leadership: 20 Case Studies to Help Ministry Leaders Adapt to Uncertainty.*

1. HOW DID YOU GET INTERESTED IN YOUR FIELD/MINISTRY?

The journey to my current ministry began with the influence of my youth pastor and his wife. I had a terrible home life and their love and care for me, and the safety I experienced in youth group, kept me close to Christ. In college I majored in youth ministry and then served at a year-round Christian camp before going to seminary for a master's in educational ministries with an emphasis in youth and family ministry.

As I continued to serve in church youth ministry, I realized that what I enjoyed most was the development of both student and adult leaders. That took me into leadership development more broadly and the pursuit of a PhD in ministry leadership so that I would be better equipped and credentialed to teach and train other ministry leaders. I also was gaining valuable experience (much of it positive, some of it very painful!) by serving alongside my husband in his pastoral ministry around the country. When I completed my doctorate, I began teaching for several schools as an adjunct instructor, which then led to expanded roles and more writing opportunities and eventually to the position I hold today.

2. HOW DID YOU PROCESS YOUR CALL?

I first received a call to vocational ministry when I was in college. I felt the Lord tell me, via inaudible but unmistakably clear words, that he wanted me to work with people in ministry, and with teenagers at that time. I had heard people talk about a "calling," such as when our church would hire a new pastor, but I didn't have much language for what I experienced at the time. I just knew it was very clear and it was from outside me, and what I heard from the Lord was accompanied by tremendous peace. Thankfully, over the next few years as I took more Bible and ministry classes, I got connected to fellow students who were on a similar journey, and to professors and student life staff who walked with us on that journey.

The harder challenge was realizing and embracing my calling and gifting as a leader, as a woman. It was okay for a female to do youth ministry, but I felt excluded from other leadership spaces. For many years, I felt something was wrong with me because I didn't fit what seemed to be the stereotype of Christian "femaleness" and especially of a pastor's wife. It wasn't until I was in my early thirties, during a wilderness period where I was wondering what was next for me after God called me out of youth ministry, that the Lord told me very clearly that I was created and called and gifted as a leader, and that I should stop paying attention to the outside voices of both men and women, and my own critical internal voice, who were trying to restrict what I was able to be, say, and do.

3. WHO HELPED YOU DISCERN YOUR CALL?

I did not grow up in a faith tradition in which one's faith community played a significant part in discerning a call. Instead, it was very individualistic. However, as a college student I had several people who affirmed my gifts. I also began to see what I was good at, loved doing, and what seemed to bring fruit and a sense of God's pleasure. By and large, though, the discernment of my call has been rooted in a lifelong process of tuning my ear to the voice of the Holy Spirit and learning to sift all other voices. I have also trusted the Lord to open and close doors to direct my path. And I seek out wise counsel, people who love me and know me well, to help discern opportunities.

4. WHAT GIVES YOU JOY AND WHAT'S MOST CHALLENGING IN YOUR WORK?

My greatest joy is being able to teach, shepherd, and encourage incredible ministry leaders—men and women who serve in churches, nonprofits, educational institutions, and itinerant and entrepreneurial ministries around the world. I learn from them as much as they do from me. In my current role, I also have the chance to shape my department's culture and bring creative leadership and input to the rest of the organization. I am very thankful that I get to bring all my education, experience, and who I am to my current work as a leader, teacher, writer, and coach.

The biggest challenge currently is that the centuries-old institutions, systems, and ways of doing things within Christianity, the church, and theological education are changing under our feet. These are the places where I have spent my entire life, and now they are all undergoing a seismic shift. I believe we are long overdue for rethinking and reconfiguring these systems and structures. It can be very unsettling at times, but also very exciting and energizing for others, to live, serve, and lead in a time of such massive disruption.

5. WHAT ADVICE DO YOU WISH SOMEONE HAD GIVEN YOU ABOUT YOUR CALL/MINISTRY?

I wish someone had told me the obstacles I would face as a female leader and a woman in ministry, and how to handle those obstacles. Some of my loudest critics have been other women, which at first was a huge surprise. I have also needed to learn how to be both fully female and fully a leader: to be fully female and not just "one of the guys" in a male-dominated world, and how to be fully a leader instead of shrinking back or hiding my gifts. Finally, I wish someone had talked to me about the importance of the responsibility to steward what God has entrusted to me. I have gifts and a call and influence and a ministry role that I must steward, and others will also be held accountable for how they stewarded my gifts and call when I was under their influence.

2
FINDING YOUR CALLING
Hannah Brown

Hannah Brown has worked as a college pastor, preaching resident, and graduate assistant. She is studying homiletics at New College, University of Edinburgh, Scotland, where she received the Parish Pulpit Fellowship in preaching.

1. HOW DID YOU GET INTERESTED IN YOUR FIELD/MINISTRY?

I decided to pursue a seminary education because of my passion for bridging the gap between the local church and academic discourse. In the future, I hope to bring these two spheres closer together, particularly in the areas of discipleship curriculum and shared preaching models. In many ways this interest has taken shape throughout my life. I fell in love with the church at an early age, and because my parents have been in ministry throughout my life, I have been afforded a unique perspective about the realities of vocational church work. I recognized early on that the church is a messy, broken, and yet profoundly beautiful place. As a kid, I frequently went on frustrated rants to my parents about problems I saw within the church and wrote sermons in my journal calling out and questioning why Christians did not act like the Jesus I knew.

In college, my faith was challenged and transformed through theological education. I learned the power of asking good questions, understood the Bible in a new way, and engaged in difficult faith conversations that reconstructed my theological framework. However, I quickly realized the transformative experience I was having through higher education was a privileged opportunity not afforded to many average church attenders. It became clear to me that the theological education I was receiving wasn't worth much if it wasn't transferable to the church and her people. This became more apparent when I started doing college ministry. I found many of the resources available to young adults either theologically shallow, with little connection to the experiences and questions they were asking, or too theologically complex, and therefore inaccessible to the average person. Recognizing this disconnection is what continues to fuel my passion for pursuing higher education.

2. HOW DID YOU PROCESS YOUR CALL?

The first time I felt God's calling on my life, I thought I was going crazy. At eleven years old, while on a mission trip with my family, I was struck with the overwhelming feeling that "this" is what I was supposed to be doing with my life. As I looked around at my previous experiences, I assumed "this" was doing mission work in some foreign country. But as I continued to grow, I started to realize that missions is everywhere: It was at church, it was on the playground at my school, it was in my friendships with others. As my dad told me once, sometimes we do not receive big, specific callings from God, but our responsibility is to put our "yes" on the table and to be obedient to the next right thing. So I began to interpret my calling as a general calling to live out my faith wherever I ended up next. I planned, believing that I was called to pursue Christ wherever I go. But God had even bigger plans for my life than that.

The summer before my senior year of high school, I was struck by an overwhelming feeling that I was making a huge mistake with my life. I felt God questioning all the plans I had made for the future and giving me a strong reminder of all the ways God had been preparing me for a life in service to the church. I was completely terrified and utterly convinced that God had made a mistake. But after months of wrestling with God, I could not shake the feeling that I needed to pursue Christian studies in higher education. I prayed that obedience to this calling would bring me more joy and fulfillment than any of my plans could.

After just a few months of studying, I fell in love with theological education. Learning in a challenging environment, where I was discovering more about God, myself, and the world every day was so fulfilling. I realized almost immediately that education is something deeply important to me, and that it would be integral to my future. I understand my work as a pastor and a student as going together. Both these spheres impact my life in significant ways and inform one another. As I looked forward to my seminary degree, I sought a learning environment that would prepare me well for both the academic and pastoral spheres.

3. WHO HELPED YOU DISCERN YOUR CALL?

For a long time, I was so scared to express my calling aloud that my parents were the only ones who knew I was discerning this calling. Fortunately, they stood by me as I discerned my calling to ministry and as I wrestled with how my plans were changing. The encouragement, support, and love they showed me in those moments was an incredible gift not afforded to every woman in ministry, and without their initial encouragement, I would not have had the courage to pursue vocational ministry.

My dad, an ordained Baptist pastor, was especially formative during those initial months of discernment. He helped me understand Baptist politics and specifically how to navigate conversations about women in ministry. He explained what happened during the "conservative resurgence" in the Southern Baptist Convention, talked about the differences between the "Baptist Faith and Message" documents, and gave me resources that aided in the discernment process. One resource that was particularly formative for me was, "Is God Calling Me?" by Jeff Iorg. While Iorg is a staunch complementarian and strictly uses male pronouns when describing pastors, it was this book that first convinced me I might be called to pastor. As Iorg described the character, motivation, and heart of a pastor, I found myself feeling seen in a way I could not describe.

As I hesitantly pursued this calling in college, it was my college pastor and professors who continued to affirm God's calling on my life. I was given opportunities to preach, was granted leadership responsibilities, and was encouraged to pursue a seminary education. There is incredible value in hearing someone say, "I think you're a leader." Receiving validation and encouragement from people you respect is such a gift. As my understanding of calling shifted to include education, the conversations I found myself having were incredibly validating. As I shared my passion for connecting the academic and church spheres, professors, peers, and coworkers alike expressed the importance of that work. Their reassurance to pursue this work and confidence in my success motivates me in my faithfulness to God's call.

4. WHAT GIVES YOU JOY AND WHAT'S MOST CHALLENGING IN YOUR WORK?

There are so many things about being a pastor and a student that bring me joy, but chief among them is the people I have the privilege of ministering to and serving with. During my time as a college minister, I was deeply transformed by the lives of the college students in my ministry. They challenged me, they asked good, hard, and holy questions, they made me laugh, and they brought me to tears more than once. Their faithfulness to God and commitment to each other continues to inspire me and challenge my own faith. I was completely unprepared for how much I would love them, and for how formative they would be for my understanding of what it means to be a pastor.

Another one of my greatest joys in ministry is preaching. As I walked away from the life I knew to prepare for a life of ministry, I prayed that my obedience to God's calling on my life would bring me more joy and fulfillment than any of my other plans could. The Lord knew that I was hardwired to preach the gospel, and every moment that I get to spend in sermon preparation and delivery is a gift. Additionally, I love the challenge of being in an academic classroom. Having difficult discussions and theologically rich conversations with peers and professors motivates me to continue learning. It is an incredible joy and privilege to study and work in a place where God has called me.

While there is so much goodness to be found in following God's calling, ministry is not for the faint of heart. Although I knew the challenges women in ministry face, I was unprepared for how isolating, disheartening, and difficult being a young woman in ministry can be. There is constant pressure, either implied or explicit, to be exceptional in everything you do. Being told that the future of women in ministry at a specific church, organization, etc., is dependent on your ability to do a good job is an unacceptable expectation to put on anyone. Additionally, constantly enduring questions about your marital status, family planning, or being asked to exegete 1 Timothy 2 is an unhealthy environment to be placed in. It can be difficult to speak up for yourself, and to often endure being dismissed, overlooked, or deemed "too difficult." Finding the balance between expressing your gratitude for the opportunities you have been given and advocating for yourself is difficult and often leaves you feeling disappointed.

5. WHAT ADVICE DO YOU WISH SOMEONE HAD GIVEN YOU ABOUT YOUR CALL/MINISTRY?

Never underestimate the power of good questions. So much of your time and energy can be wasted on searching for certainty. Obsession with being right or finding the right answers misses the beauty of asking good questions. So often, God is found in the ambiguity, and we miss what God is doing because we are consumed with what we do not understand. In the pursuit of being right, we often forget to be faithful where we are. Life is messy and so often does not have easy explanations. Rather than trying to make everything easily understandable, embrace the fullness of life by growing comfortable with the unknown.

You are not responsible for other people's expectations. People will have expectations or assumptions about what it means for you to be a woman or a young person in ministry. But your calling is not to fulfill others' expectations; your calling is to Christ. God made you incredibly unique and invites you to partner in kingdom work just as you are. God does not work despite you but chooses to work through you. So, embrace all the things that make you unique, and trust that God did not make a mistake in calling you to the task at hand. Your ministry will suffer if you spend all your time trying to be and do what others expect. Yes, seek and take wise advice, collaborate, and embrace people with kindness, but never let another person's expectations of you dictate how you respond to God's calling in your life.

Doing something for yourself is not selfish. Taking time to rest and recenter yourself is the only way you will survive in ministry. Fight hard to protect your time of rest and do not sacrifice your sanity for anything. You are allowed to say "no" to good things for the sake of protecting your own spiritual, physical, and mental well-being. If you do not take time for yourself, your body will eventually force you to slow down. And if your current situation becomes unhealthy, you are allowed to walk away from it, knowing that your well-being is important to God. Being a leader means modeling good practices, and it is irresponsible leadership to never allow yourself rest.

3
FINDING YOUR CALLING
Mariah Humphries

Mariah Humphries is a Mvskoke Nation citizen with German, Scottish, and Czech heritage. Her published works can be found online and in books, including *Need to Know* and *Voices of Lament*.

1. HOW DID YOU GET INTERESTED IN YOUR FIELD/MINISTRY?

My field of work is writing and speaking on the intersection of racialized identities and Christianity. It is formed by a combination of my lived experience and a missing voice in my sphere of influence. In the work of biblical justice there is a gap for Native Christians, especially women, to speak on the historical and current role the church has held in the history of the United States and the opportunity to correct and lead the path toward healing. I saw that need and stepped in to fill part of that gap and remain in this work because of my love for the church. For me, to love something deeply means I believe in it, but there is also accountability that comes with that love. My support for the church is not fading anytime soon, but it needs to be aware, acknowledge its actions against communities of color, and lead the path toward healing.

I grew up knowing and witnessing both Native men and boys as well as women and girls who were victims of societal bias and racism. Some were friends and relatives, and it brought injustice to the forefront for me as a child and into my adulthood. I had assumed systemic injustice was primarily toward Native people because that was my experience. The reality of the experience of the Black community came to the forefront in 2012 with the killing of Trayvon Martin.

Between 2012 and the fall of 2016, I became increasingly discouraged and disappointed in the American Christian church as police shootings, anti-Asian hate acts, and treatment of Latinos/Latinas along our border and in our communities, combined with treatment of Native peoples, were in our headlines. Christians were anemic in speaking out against these injustices and that is where I knew I needed to speak on the actions affecting the Native community and support brown and Black voices who also brought awareness to the masses.

I found myself being asked to speak more about the inhumane actions taken against brown and Black bodies. Sometimes this was based on what I had witnessed and at times it was based on statistics that had been released. As I developed as a writer and speaker, I knew researching history would be essential to my work, and so would a deeper understanding of scripture.

I have always loved writing since I was a young girl, but I was not one to speak with confidence. I was very introverted and public speaking or teaching was not on my bingo card! As I look back now, my first interest in writing sprouted from watching my mother lead others, which included how she held herself in the public eye as both an educator and the spouse of a pastor.

My mother was a professor of English. She was always writing curriculum and reading and studying. As a Mvskoke woman, she was also one of the women, *and Native women*, who broke through the glass ceiling of male-dominated higher education. She became one of the first female professors at Haskell Indian Junior College, now Haskell Indian Nations University. She had a clear passion—I would say a calling—to use her giftedness to serve her own people by teaching Native students. I feel my call is similar by using my giftedness to bring awareness of my people to non-Native spaces.

Her time in higher education would be cut short. During her pregnancy with me she was diagnosed with rheumatoid arthritis, which eventually became terminal. When her disease became severe, she knew she needed to step away from her position as a professor. Wheelchair-bound and navigating a new life she never considered, she remained a teacher to those who needed one. She led Bible studies, discipled countless people over the decades, taught Sunday school, and while we lived on a reservation in Nevada, she became a GED educator for the Walker River Paiute Tribe.

American society would view her as fragile and incapable due to her physical appearance, but her physical journey did not deter her work as a writer and educator. In fact, it opened the door for her to become a significant person in others' lives. Her journey of walking through doors that needed someone to enter became my foundation for discovering my calling in life.

2. HOW DID YOU PROCESS YOUR CALL?

Entering rooms that lacked representation is where I found my place in this work called justice. I reflect on my mother's example of taking on the obstacles in front of her and it challenges me to look beyond how society views my identities and bring confidence that only the Holy Spirit could provide at times. The calling of speaking and writing for the education of others, not just for myself, has been a process of years and although I am confident in my gifts now, processing is still part of a lifelong calling.

A foundational part of my work is staying true to scripture. There is a lot of misuse and weaponization of the actions of Jesus and scripture, in our Christian spaces, and it is imperative we stay the course when it comes to injustice and pursuing justice. Early in my work I witnessed a lot of voices speaking but not staying rooted in their faith and I wanted to make my faith stronger, not weaker, so I decided to attend seminary. I felt it was important for me to establish my knowledge of scripture, theology, and practical application to confidently challenge and encourage other Christians.

Honestly, there was a moment of hesitation since I was not on a traditional student route, I was a brown-skinned woman, and I was older than most students. Earlier, in my twenties, I had witnessed older seminary students being treated with dismissiveness by their younger peers. These all brought moments of doubt as I considered my place in this sacred space of seminary. With those considered, I still felt called to attend to be theologically sound as I moved forward in life.

3. WHO HELPED YOU DISCERN YOUR CALL?

Our call is our own, but I believe others will see that calling in our actions and character. My husband was my primary advocate in my decision to attend seminary, and our children, teenagers at the time, were in full support of me. Although I did not announce my seminary admittance to too many, those within my inner circle provided confirmation as I shared my decision with them. There is a peace that you experience when you know this call is from God, but it is deepened when your "people" affirm that calling.

One of the most significant voices for me in discerning my field of work was while I was already attending seminary. Dr. Lai-Ling "Elizabeth" Ngan was a vocal advocate for my call. I will never forget taking her notorious final exam and when I completed it, she looked at me and said, "Good job, Mariah. You did well, but now let's talk." She spent the remaining time encouraging me and challenging me to remain strong as I graduated. As we had already discussed throughout the semester, she knew I was facing and would continue to face obstacles as a brown-skinned woman educating Christian men and women that would not look like me. We discussed the pushback brown women faced when they step forward to fill gaps or take on a leadership role. Outside of my family, she was the most significant voice in discerning the path I was taking.

4. WHAT GIVES YOU JOY AND WHAT'S MOST CHALLENGING IN YOUR WORK?

I was part of the 2020 non-graduation ceremony graduates. Rather than walk across the stage with my family in the crowd to watch me receive my diploma, I sat in a Zoom call with professors and other 2020 graduates. The question I will always remember came from a spiritual formation professor. She asked us how they could pray for us. My answer was simple: for me to remain theologically sound as I stepped into a world that was trying its best to challenge the connection of scripture to justice and shake my foundation.

Receiving a master's in theology, I knew I would gain more respect from many, but my racialized identity would continue to be a roadblock for many men and women. That is a challenge at times. It is hard on your body and mind. It can question your faith in fellow Christians. Words like justice, equality, and equity have become such divisive words in our churches and I believe it is a direct reflection of allowing external entities to enter our faith spaces. Anytime the church allows an empire mindset to sway kingdom focus, the result is chaos.

The challenge is to remain ready and grace-filled with every conversation. To know when to walk away from someone and when to push them out of their comfort zone. That is also the joy; when you see hearts changed and mindsets open to really live out Micah 6:8. Joy in knowing I am following the steps of Native Christian women before me, like my mother, and knowing I am a product of their sacrifice, calling, and work. Using my voice, and my faith, to change the world I live in, with the hope of leaving it better than when I entered it.

5. WHAT ADVICE DO YOU WISH SOMEONE HAD GIVEN YOU ABOUT YOUR CALL/MINISTRY?

Remember, your faith is yours and yours alone. It is not the faith of your parent, pastor, spouse, or friend. In the same vein, this is your call/ministry and yours alone. Remain confident in that calling. Seminary can be difficult in ways you are not expecting, and our calling is the grounding we have as we face those difficulties.

Broaden your opinion and expectation of what ministry or calling looks like. If you are called to step into a pastoral position, that is great. Go out into the church and make it better. But if you feel called to be a chaplain, professor, writer, counselor, social worker, lawyer, director of a nonprofit, or musician, that is a ministry too. The legitimacy of your call to ministry is not determined by what title you hold. Although seminary education still leans heavily on the pastoral staff position, there are many of us who make an impact outside of the traditional path of ministry. If you are in seminary, challenge your fellow seminarians and professors to address, or perhaps accept, ministry roles outside the traditional box.

Please, do not be afraid to ask questions once you have sought out answers on your own. One of the best ways to gauge your knowledge is to ask questions. I ask questions to colleagues and friends of different identities and experiences all the time, especially as a leader. Asking questions, verbal or written, is a way to discern if you are grasping and learning. If you want to expand, questions must be asked. There will be times you feel embarrassed by your question and that is okay. Ask anyway. There are times when you receive pushback from a professor, leader, or peer. Ask anyway. You may not have affirmation or clarity if you keep your questions internal.

I will say this: Go out and do the hard work. Your voice is needed. The church needs you, and our society needs you.

4
FINDING YOUR CALLING
Memory Jora

Memory Jora is former program manager of the Kyle Lake Center for Effective Preaching at Truett Seminary and currently serves as Executive Director at The Church Without Walls in Houston, Texas. She is currently working on her Doctorate in Ministry degree at Gordon-Conwell Theological Seminary in Art, Ministry and Mission.

1. HOW DID YOU GET INTERESTED IN YOUR FIELD/MINISTRY?

I personally believe that for me the interest came about through a series of divine disruptions, which led me to a life of ministry. Before then, I had not been inclined to pursue a ministry life and was content with my fashion and business career. However, through some unexplainable circumstances (divine disruptions) the burning desire for me to dedicate the rest of my life serving God through ministry set a fire in me that changed the trajectory of my life. At that time, I was not sure what that decision to go into ministry truly entailed beyond a surrendered heart. So, even discerning which field of ministry I would go into was not that apparent to me then. That revelation keeps unraveling as I continue to be open to God's will and to be faithfully present wherever he plants me.

A calling, theologically, is the sense of a specific vision for how God wants us to live our lives, serving him by inspiring people and meeting human needs in his kingdom. In my case, discovering my calling and interest in ministry has not been a one-time event. It has been something that continues to unfold with time even beyond typical ministry settings.

2. HOW DID YOU PROCESS YOUR CALL?

I think for me, being that I am only four years into my ministry calling, I am still processing the call. My call continues to be an ever-evolving journey which I navigate every day to the best of my abilities. I take 2 Corinthians 5:7 very literally, in which the apostle Paul says, "We walk by faith, not by sight" (NKJV). So, as I continue to process my call, I strive to lean not on my own understanding but in my faith about what God said when he redirected my life towards ministry.

Beyond being a lifelong student of the "Word," one way I process my call is through the spiritual discipline of a prayer. Prayer is how I can partner with the Holy Spirit through my words about the will of God over my life. I can bring my circumstances, petition, struggles, or hardships to God through prayer. Prayer enables me to focus on the glory and goodness of God and not on my issues. This helps me to navigate my call forward when emotions, discouragement, and the pressures of ministry start to cloud my judgment and the temptation to give up arises. It is therefore especially important for me on this ministry journey not to have an idealized but a practical and realistic view of myself, my capabilities, my giftings, and the type of ministry that God has called me to serve in. Being fully aware and accepting of all these facets of myself allows me to pursue roles that I am adequately equipped and trained for, as well as to continue to develop myself, so that I can reach my maximum potential. I love learning and I try to constantly remind myself that one should never get to a place in their call where they feel like they know everything or have arrived.

With each new experience along the way, I continue to realize that everyone's call to ministry is going to be oriented differently, both in terms of what that means on a personal level as well as what it means season to season. In my case, with each new experience or season that I have encountered or been confronted with thus far, I have found myself being challenged so differently in ways that have often required distinct aspects of me which I did not even realize I had in me. These have often felt like new personal discoveries in myself and the giftings God bestowed in me prior to the call.

3. WHO HELPED YOU DISCERN YOUR CALL?

I have been able to process my call through leaning into the wise counsel of mentors that I look up to, such as former professors, the local church, family, and some of my peers, all of whom are invested in and supportive of my ministry calling. Sometimes they have helped me to identify certain blind spots I would have missed about myself, situations, or about ministry opportunities I would be considering.

While still in seminary school, the opportunity that allowed me to serve on staff at Concord Church in Dallas through Truett Seminary's ministry residence program, as well as working as a college ministry associate at First Baptist Church Arlington, were all very instrumental to the discernment and shaping of my ministry call. At Concord Church, Pastor Aaron Moore, who throughout the residency program was my spiritual mentor, as well as Pastor Austin Medley, to whom I directly reported in youth ministry, perfected my understanding of homiletics, community, and the importance of spiritual formation in ministry, as well as showing me what it means to faithfully serve in an assignment no matter the circumstances.

What I learned from them was that there is a preeminence of the call over your feelings, even though how we often feel about things is valid. Endurance in ministry requires a steady pace of taking each moment or crisis as it comes and trusting that God is in control. We are the vessels through which the kingdom of God is realized on earth. So, we must model to others what that looks like through our different ministries no matter the challenges.

At First Baptist Arlington college ministry, working alongside Connor Torrealba, the college ministry director, was monumental in shaping my passion for contextual exegesis, as well as in helping me gain new insights on the importance of evangelism in ministry.

I will also add to the list of those who have influenced my call, Todd Still, dean of Truett Seminary; Pastor Brian Carter, head pastor of Concord Church; and Jo Ann Reinowski, director of advising at Truett Seminary. Their leadership styles in ministry and commitment to excellence in everything that I watch them do has been so inspirational to my call. Through watching them, I am able to discern that God has also called me to execute that level of excellence in everything that I do. So, whatever I do, I must do it all for the glory of God with a standard of nothing but excellence.

Currently in my call I am grateful for Dr. Matthew Kim, Dr. Jared Alcántara, and Rev. Kenneth McNeil, and for how their influence, mentorship, guidance, and support are impacting my call in ministry, as well as shaping me as a person. I am confident that God sent them into this season of my life for a specific reason: to help prepare, shape, and equip me for whatever is next on this journey of the call. So, being in community with others can be a great way to learn and discern God's will over your life. We are not meant to do ministry all by ourselves in isolation. Ministry requires community!

4. WHAT GIVES YOU JOY AND WHAT IS MOST CHALLENGING IN YOUR WORK?

One of the most challenging things about being in ministry/my work is that it is extremely hard to define what success looks like because that differs for everyone. I work at the intersection of academia and the church, so defining ministry success from that context is especially challenging. Despite the challenge, to me ministry success is being able to foster relationships with other people in a way that impacts their spiritual formation, ultimately pointing them to Christ, who in turn transforms them no matter their situation or circumstances. Impacting others in this way, which allows them to see themselves as God's image bearers, brings me so much joy. Relationship formation and presence is paramount to my call. I know that I cannot build meaningful relationships with people unless I am grounded and faithfully present in all the moments that I am privileged to engage with them. Thus, being able to connect with others on a deep level, where they feel affirmed, heard, and seen is something I strive to do every day through my work.

5. WHAT ADVICE DO YOU WISH SOMEONE HAD GIVEN YOU ABOUT YOUR CALL/MINISTRY?

I wish someone had told me that it would not be easy, and that some days I would want to give up. I wish they had also told me that I would have to constantly remind myself of my first love, Jesus, the whole reason I am in ministry. I say this because I constantly need this reminder when the busyness of work starts consuming all my time and robs me of my devotional time with him.

I also wish that someone had told me that despite one of the local church's missions, from a universal church's standpoint, being to draw people to Christ, that is often something which is only understood in theory and not in practice by most congregations. From a convening standpoint, most churches struggle with formulating the necessary structures to create and foster an environment which draws and retains people from diverse cultural backgrounds. Yet as believers, we have all been called to exercise the Great Commission wherever we are.

5

FINDING YOUR CALLING

Shelby Livingstone

Shelby Livingstone is an assistant volleyball coach at Baylor University and a former student athlete at Rice University.

1. HOW DID YOU GET INTERESTED IN YOUR FIELD/MINISTRY?

It was the last day of volleyball practice before spring break, my junior year at Rice University. I jumped to hit the ball, as I had hundreds of times in my volleyball career, but this attack ended differently. When I landed, all my weight on my left leg, I immediately crumbled to the floor, heard a pop in my left knee, and felt excruciating pain. I knew something was very wrong. After doctors' visits and lots of tears, I learned I had torn my ACL and meniscus, news that led to a nine-month recovery and lots of heartache. However, through this devastating injury and bump in the road of my volleyball career, being forced to take nine months away from the sport I had placed my identity in, I had the chance to reevaluate my purpose and, in turn, to begin the start of my journey of finding my true calling in ministry.

Sports have always been a major part of my life. I grew up playing almost every sport imaginable and had two parents and two grandfathers who all played basketball collegiately. I always knew I wanted to play college volleyball, and that drive allowed me to play Division 1 volleyball at Rice University in Houston, Texas. My whole life I loved sports and I loved Jesus, but I had never truly taken the time to understand how those two passions could work together. I was living my life as a Christian and as an athlete but the two never fully crossed paths—at least not, as mentioned above, until the spring of my junior year of college when I tore my ACL and meniscus and what I loved most in life, volleyball, was taken from me.

For nine months of recovery, I could no longer place my identity in volleyball, my stat line, or what my coaches thought of me. Nine months outside of volleyball gave me time to rethink my "why" of being an athlete and allowed me to recenter my identity and passion on Christ. It allowed me to reclaim the sport of volleyball as an avenue of worship instead of the sole thing I placed my worth in. After having this experience, recovering, and being given the chance to play an extra year of college volleyball at Rice, I knew I was passionate about staying in the world of college athletics and I wanted to empower college athletes to know that they are more than just their stat line. I knew I wanted to invest in the broken world of college athletics. Sports can hold so much good and joy in their created form, but in our fallen world this is not how we experience sports every day. I know from my personal story as an athlete that the world of college athletics can be dark, lonely, and seemingly meaningless at times. It was clear in my life that the Lord was calling me to invest back into the lives of as many college athletes as possible.

2. HOW DID YOU PROCESS YOUR CALL?

I understood I had a call from the Lord on my life to enter sports ministry, but I could not begin to understand how that would be possible. That is, until I was looking at graduate degrees at Baylor University and stumbled across Truett Seminary's master of divinity with a concentration in sports ministry. I immediately knew this was the next step for me to continue to faithfully and confidently walk in this call on my life. I did not know a lot going into the program, but I knew I loved Jesus, I loved sports, and I loved school. Truett felt like a perfect fit.

I stepped out in faith, trusting that going to seminary, diving deeper into studying theology and understanding my personal faith, and gaining a greater understanding of how to integrate faith and sports would continue to prepare me well for a future in sports ministry. Truett Seminary and the sports ministry concentration did just that by introducing me to like-minded professors and future ministers who invested in my life, not just as a student, but as a friend, knowing me by name and taking the effort to learn my story. At Truett, I was not just another face in the crowd, but rather, an integrated part of the loving, caring, and compassionate community focused on championing all who feel called to ministry.

3. WHO HELPED YOU DISCERN YOUR CALL?

While my injury in college was the first step in beginning to process and understand my call, Truett Seminary was my second step in processing my call. The cherry on top of discerning and fully embracing the Lord's call on my life in ministry was my friends, family, professors, and pastors who were championing me the entire way and confidently speaking life into my work as I dove headfirst into ministry with college athletes. It is true when they say, "It takes a village." My village equipped and prepared me in ways I did not even understand at the time to never question my call, especially my call as a woman in ministry.

I am forever grateful for the women in my life, specifically the female preachers of the Baptist church I grew up in, that showed me firsthand what it looks like to be a woman called to ministry. These women—Julie Pennington-Russell, Mary Alice Birdwhistell, and Hannah Coe—created a ministry environment that never made me question a woman's call to preach, teach, and lead behind the pulpit and in whatever ministry context they were called to. I come from a place of privilege in the Baptist Church because I grew up seeing female pastors lead and preach in the most eloquent and heaven-shaking ways I have ever experienced in the church. I am unable to express the depth of my gratitude for these women and the church leadership at Calvary Baptist Church in Waco, Texas, for allowing me to grow up in an affirming and empowering environment that invaluably impacted my call in ways I did not even understand growing up but which I am forever enriched to have known.

I am indebted to these women who bore more hardships than I could ever imagine and showed young girls like me that our call to preach and lead in churches is not wrong but rather, divinely ordained. Women like Julie, Mary, Hannah, and my mom, Linda Livingstone, helped me discern my call almost subconsciously. They allowed me to see them lead in glass ceiling–shattering ways that never made me question the Lord's call on my life to pursue ministry, whether that was in a church behind a pulpit or in the gym with a whistle in hand.

4. WHAT GIVES YOU JOY AND WHAT'S MOST CHALLENGING IN YOUR WORK?

I love being a coach because it is a title that allows me access to student athletes in ways many others cannot. It is a title that allows me to live through the joys as well as the hardships of some of the most formative and difficult years of their lives while trying to balance school, sports, and their social lives. Playing volleyball at Rice, being the volunteer assistant at Baylor University, and most recently serving as an assistant coach at Liberty University, I have been given a front-row seat and have experienced firsthand the highest of highs of college athletics as well as the lowest of lows that come with being a student athlete. Sport, in its best form, can be used as an amazing form of worship, but many times, this is not how it is experienced or used. The dark underbelly of sports and college athletics many times feels as if there is no hope and no light for Christ in a world full of deceit, manipulation, and pain. That is why it is so important for Christian athletes, coaches, and sports ministers to continue to shine the light of Christ and help bring sport back to its worshipful, created purpose.

One of the most amazing and worshipful moments I have ever experienced in sports happened, surprisingly, after a Baylor volleyball loss in the Final Four match against Wisconsin in 2019. It was a magical season for our team, which I was a part of as the volunteer assistant coach. We went into the tournament as the number one overall ranked seed in the country. Expectations were high and sights were set on a national championship. The dream journey ended in Wisconsin. However, the story of the Baylor team's impact for the Lord that year did not end with the defeat to Wisconsin. Instead, after the match, as the Baylor team does after every match, the players asked to pray with the Wisconsin team. This moment was powerful for the players on the court, but we learned later that ESPN had aired the prayer in full on the postgame broadcast. As the Baylor and Wisconsin players circled up arm in arm on the court, tens of thousands of people were hearing the gospel on ESPN from this prayer. Hundreds of thousands more people were able to listen to it as it circulated around social media in the days and weeks following Baylor's loss.

Moments like this are what sports, and being a Christian in sports, are all about. The Baylor volleyball players were a light even after a loss, not just to their opponent, but to the entire country and everyone who tuned in to ESPN that night. The joy of my position as coach and minister to college athletes is the opportunity to know the young women on my teams, like these Baylor players. Knowing their stories and their successes and triumphs brings me more joy than any on-court success. I want my athletes to feel loved as more than just an athlete but as a daughter, student, sister, and friend.

In many ways it is also a joy and privilege to sit with athletes through moments of sadness, defeat, injury, hurt, and pain. I find these moments to be some of the most holy. Being invited into the most vulnerable pieces of a student athlete's life is something I will never take for granted. I hope to always use these moments to sit with them in their pain and, in the right timing, point them to Christ and make sure they know they are not alone with their struggles. I hope to show my athletes that there is power and strength from the Lord in vulnerability, not shame and rejection as they are often led to believe.

5. WHAT ADVICE DO YOU WISH SOMEONE HAD GIVEN YOU ABOUT YOUR CALL/MINISTRY?

When looking to my call to ministry, a call I continue to discern daily, I wish someone had told me earlier to "take up space." I wish I had leaned into my call more confidently and unwaveringly in college ministry because I know the women who have come before me would want nothing less from me. I wish I had not allowed those who do not know me or what I see in the public sphere to influence me away from my calling. I wish someone in college had told me that the most important thing in my first job once I graduated was not how big my paycheck is.

I hope to tell the women who come after me to take up the mantle that women like Julie Pennington-Russell, Mary Alice Birdwhistell, and Hannah Coe have so powerfully and rightfully passed on so that the next generation of young girls who feel called to ministry will have no doubt in their mind that they are able to preach, teach, and lead in the same way men are. I hope to continue to pass on the legacy these women imparted to me so that the next generation of young girls will never question whether they are called to ministry because that is all they know—women behind the pulpit stepping confidently into their call.

6
FINDING YOUR CALLING

Melanie Pacheco

Melanie Pacheco is a first-generation Latina of Dominican and Peruvian descent who was born and raised in New Jersey. She is a campus ministry associate at Baylor University.

1. HOW DID YOU GET INTERESTED IN YOUR FIELD/MINISTRY?

His love was a song that began as the soundtrack to my life. It was constant, but initially its sound was only found in the periphery. As I grew up in church, the song became a familiar tune that my mind knew well. When I was eight years of age, the echoing began. I could imitate every melisma of the song, every drum fill, the ebbs and flows of the bassline, the chord progression of the keys, and even the ad-libs. As if that was not enough, he even gave me a voice to sing it right back to him. This shifted one day—I cannot tell you exactly when—but I realized his melody was a traveling one. This meant that it could not be constrained by the background or contained in my limited mind. His voice, whether booming or soothing, CARRIES. The words it utters accomplish what they set out to do. In my case, the song became clearer, so much so that what my mind recognized initially, my heart was now attuned to. I was seduced. You see, he began to sing something I had never heard before. He explained that what I echoed all these years was only the intro. Woven in the verses that would follow were sweet melodies of deliverance, identity, and love. That revelation served as an invitation to adventure into unknown territories of his heart and subsequently my own. The Lord invited me to be molded by him, to follow him, and to know him. More than just an interest in this field or ministry, he has quickly consumed me. I can join in with the psalmist's proclamation saying, "Because Your love is better than life, my lips will glorify You. I will praise You as long as I live and in Your name I will lift my hands" (Psalm 63:3–4, NIV).

2. HOW DID YOU PROCESS YOUR CALL?

The basement of my childhood home housed many keepsake boxes. Inside them were pictures of all kinds, which I enjoyed looking through periodically. You could find photographed memories that captured anything and everything from my mother's fifteenth birthday to the day my baby brother was brought home from the hospital. One evening as I sorted through them, one picture of my parents rehearsing for Sunday service worship caught my eye. My godmother, another worship leader, would always tell me that they practiced in front of mostly empty pews except for a baby carrier. Within it was me all wide-eyed and bundled up against the New Jersey winter. I was exposed to ministry before I knew my own name. It is a mercy and a grace that the Lord would open my eyes to see his details, such as these, displayed so evidently in my life. His call is intentional and deeply personal. I, like all followers of Christ, am called to love God above all else and to love people as myself. There are assignments attached to my call that shift and change according to my location, my giftings, and areas of my heart and life that the Lord prompts me to be growing in at any given moment. Recently, that looked like leading a campus ministry in Texas and prioritizing entering the Lord's rest. In the future, it could mean raising a family elsewhere or continuing my academic studies. Whatever the case may be, understanding this distinction has been my key to processing vocational ministry in a healthy way without taking it up as the entirety of my identity. Also, it helps to establish a habit of living surrendered to all the Lord has planned even when it has been surprising or unsettling to me in the past.

3. WHO HELPED YOU DISCERN YOUR CALL?

It was my father who first called me his princess and then a leader. It was my mother who was the first to show me what a true woman of God that edifies her house looks like. It was my brother who first called me "pastor" and then actually let me pastor him (unbeknownst to me at the time). I could go down a list of leaders, mentors, teachers, and friends who all helped me through the discernment process. But I mention the first three because not only are they the people who know me best, but they are the ones that God constantly uses to remind me who I am. This has been especially instrumental in my darkest moments when my sin tries to convince me that I am not the daughter of the King or on the days when I wake up too tired to serve or on the long nights where lies beg my mind to doubt the Lord's call. In these moments I remember the truth given by the one who created me into my most intimate circle.

Above all else, partnership with the Holy Spirit is imperative to my discernment process. The most fruitful time spent with him is filled with conversing and listening. He has led me to places I am meant to be with the appointed people at the appointed time.

4. WHAT GIVES YOU JOY AND WHAT'S MOST CHALLENGING IN YOUR WORK?

Being a vessel in God's hands gives me joy. For example, I love to see people connect with God when they can resonate with a sermon illustration or lesson point that I am teaching. Additionally, I am honored that people would trust me to offer sound spiritual direction and confide the intimate details of their life to me because they feel safe enough to do so. I recognize that all credit and glory belong to God for these ministry opportunities. I do not take it lightly that God has chosen to place his treasure in this imperfect, earthen vessel or that he would choose to make me a dwelling place for his Holy Spirit. My mind cannot understand it fully, but I have come to accept that sharing in his victory as his daughter permits me to partake in this very good work.

Simultaneously, being a vessel in God's hands is the most challenging part of my work. I must recommit to staying on the potter's wheel daily. As the potter, he reserves the right to mold, cut, crush, add, or take away all that he sees fit until he reaches the intended design. This is painful and difficult to endure, but there are no shortcuts. This type of processing produces character, which is the catalyst for effective and lasting ministry work. All I can do is ask God for his strength and company as he works on my heart.

5. WHAT ADVICE DO YOU WISH SOMEONE HAD GIVEN YOU ABOUT YOUR CALL/MINISTRY?

As women, the Lord chose to crown creation with us to bring forth beauty, to be of support, to bear life, and to minister to his heart. All these functions are opposed by the enemy. His aims to steal, kill, and destroy are the opposite of our purpose which is why the feminine heart is constantly under attack. This means that being a woman in ministry requires so much bravery. Just ask Deborah, who had to lead the people of God into war. A woman must be valiant to truly believe that everything that outside voices determine as weakness (ex: being vulnerable with emotions, being nurturing) is the unique framework which God has provided for us to worship and serve him. Just ask Hannah, who was deemed drunk and crazy because of the intensity with which she prayed as she expressed her desire and need before the Lord. As women in ministry, there is something special about the way we worship.

We touch God's heart with the posture of our own. Just ask the woman with the blood flow or Mary as she anointed Christ. They bowed physically so their outer bodies could reflect the position of their hearts: humble and faith filled. A woman that wants to please God with her life is a woman of prayer that seeks intimacy with God and is unashamed to come boldly before his throne to remain at his feet. It is in the secret place that God gives the comfort for the heartache that ministry brings, reassurance for the days where one hears *again* that women cannot preach/teach/ fill-in-the-blank, and strategy for where to go or what to do next, if anything. May he find us faithful, stewarding everything he has placed in our hands excellently, and loving on his people for the glory of his Name and the building of his kingdom.

II
Calling in Church Ministry

7
EXECUTIVE PASTOR
Jenni Wong Clayville

Jenni Wong Clayville serves as the Executive Pastor at NoVA Community Church and the Leading and Loving It and Propel Ecclesia teams, supporting women in ministry internationally.

1. HOW DID YOU GET INTERESTED IN YOUR FIELD/MINISTRY?

"What do you want to be when you grow up?" I looked up from the weed I was pulling in the front yard. My mother, who was diligently pulling weeds a couple of feet away from me, had broken me out of my slightly hypnotic stance from the *stab-stab-pull* rhythm of my weeding tool.

I was fourteen or fifteen years old and knew I was *called*, though I did not have the language to describe it yet. I had been attending an immigrant church since I was three, when my godmother introduced my mother to Jesus and the church. I am forever grateful to my godmother for how she actively changed my family's life trajectory. I accepted Jesus as the Savior of my life early on and was baptized as a young teenager. Even in the ebb and flow of adolescence and young adulthood, I was confident in who Christ was and that I was meant to do kingdom work.

However, in my context, I never saw women in ministry, much less Chinese American women in ministry. The only women I had ever seen on the platform or in service were background vocalists on the worship team, choir members, or women who served in the children's ministry. Of course, there was the singular pastor's wife who supported her husband in ministry, and her role seemed closest to what I felt God created me to do.

2. HOW DID YOU PROCESS YOUR CALL?

So, to my mother's question, I responded: "I want to be a pastor's wife."

I was born and raised in Seattle, Washington, by immigrant parents from Hong Kong. I am Chinese American, and English is my second language, after Cantonese. I didn't learn to speak English effectively until well into elementary school, but that is a story for another book. I am the eldest of three daughters and the eldest of all my cousins. There are many nuances to this birth order mixed with Chinese, American, and Christian cultures. My second-generation immigrant childhood was far from easy as I incessantly stood in the tension of the "in-between liminality" of cultures in America—Chinese, American, female, and Christian.

My parents divorced when I was seven, leaving all three of us with my mother. My father did not feel resourced enough to care for his children. My mother was disconnected and emotionally unavailable at best, but more realistically, abusive. "Home" was an unsafe place. I do not doubt that my parents loved me and did their best with what they had, but I also understand that their best was abysmal. One can imagine the effect this had on how I must have viewed my heavenly Father based on the actions (or lack thereof) of my earthly parents.

3. WHO HELPED YOU DISCERN YOUR CALL?

Higher education is what sparked me to life. I went on to study psychology as it animated and linked all the disconnects in my personal and professional life. These ideas brought meaning and understanding to daily situations and to how the full spectrum of human personalities responded to life and culture. Not a day has gone by that I haven't put into practice something I learned from my psychology degrees. Continued study in psychology even presented a clear path to grace for my parents that brought personal healing and hope. I later added a graduate degree in theology that furthered a more holistic understanding of the wholeness in which God created humanity to thrive.

My studies only propelled my desire, and I felt a *calling* toward vocational ministry. Honestly, I think I "accidentally" fell into vocational ministry ("accidentally" from my view—but we all know God does things purposefully). I would never have thought to apply for a pastoral position at a church, but I was well into volunteering in worship ministry at this point. However, someone in a place of power saw my potential early on and helped create a previously nonexistent leadership position in the church for me. This person helped me start my vocational ministry career when women in ministry were unpopular, and I did not yet understand how to advocate for myself. This was over twenty-five years ago. I am beyond grateful for the many allies in my life.

In my early years in vocational ministry, I struggled with teaching and living out a life that revealed a gracious triune God. Knowing you are called is different than understanding *why* you are *called*. My misunderstanding of this concept, mixed with my tragic identity issues, only complicated the matter. The only way to comprehend our God-given identity is by understanding where our identity is created. Let's dive into this a bit through what Scripture tells us about God.

First, there is God the Father. In Luke, in the parable of the lost sheep, lost coin, and prodigal son, we see the Father not sending a servant out but instead going out himself to recover his lost, strayed, and suffering children. He leaves the ninety-nine for the one (Luke 15:2–7). Our God sweeps the house on hands and knees, looking in every nook and cranny for that *one* coin because it holds value (Luke 15:8–10). And our loving Father waits outside his home, looking in the distance for the child who has abandoned him and squandered his inheritance (Luke 15:11–32).

In Luke 15:20 (NIV), we read, "But while he was still a long way off, his father saw him and was filled with compassion for him; he ran to his son, threw his arms around him and kissed him." We are discovering here that the Father is not distant and far off. Instead, the Father is waiting in love and anticipation for us despite what we have done to offend him. This picture illustrated by Jesus is the opposite of my personal experience with my mother, which meant I needed to do the work required to change the narrative of who God the Father is in my life.

Next is God the Son. John 1:1 (NIV) reads, "In the beginning was the Word, and the Word was with God, and the Word was God." The Word, translated from the Greek word *logos*, implies the divine. The Word is Jesus Christ, as he was with God from the very beginning.

And from that, in Philippians 2, Paul explains the reason for Jesus coming to earth in what is referred to as the christological hymn—Jesus, the only Son of God, leaves preexistent glory to come be with humanity, and in doing this, Jesus trades his highest divine honor to become the lowliest of humans, *to die a slave's death*. Christ then pours himself out in his humiliation, calling for a paradigm vindication. In other words, the paradigm is the call for all believers to *go and do likewise*.

Instead of elevating himself, the Son lives out and brings forth the kingdom of God by sharing his life on earth.

He fellowships and befriends the outcast.

He restores the broken.

He advocates for the marginalized.

He dines and celebrates with those determined unworthy of community.

He chooses to be in proximity to the sick, forgotten, and most threatened.

And in all this, Jesus reveals a communion between Father and Son instead of doing it all alone. Jesus coming to earth is Immanuel, God with us.

But wait, there's more. Rounding out the three-in-one is God the Spirit. In John 14:16 (NRSVue), Jesus says, "And I will ask the

Father, and he will give you another Advocate, to be with you forever." John 15:26 reads, "When the Advocate comes, whom I will send to you from the Father, the Spirit of truth who comes from the Father, he will testify on my behalf."

The Holy Spirit in Judaism is referred to as *Ruach HaKodesh* (*Ruach* means "spirit," "wind," or "breath," and *kodesh* means "holy"). The *Ruach HaKodesh* is present with us because God loves us so much that he not only gave us Jesus but also an Advocate.

The *Holy Spirit* comes from the *Father* at the request of the *Son*, and now *we* have access to the *Father* because *Jesus* sent the *Holy Spirit* to *us* on behalf of the *Father*. As confusing as that may be, understanding what the persons of God in community with each other look like is essential. How we view the Trinity matters because we are the literal reflection—the Imago Dei—the image of God. Let's dive even deeper.

Ruach HaKodesh is a feminine term. Also, Yahweh (translated into "I AM WHO I AM," the first name we knew to call God) can be broken into two parts: "yah" = feminine and "weh" = masculine. Why am I bringing this up? Great question. I'm so glad you asked. Because knowing the feminine in God affects how we see and care for the feminine in our community. Remembering that Jesus came down from preexisting glory to serve and die a slave's death affects how we see the most marginalized in our community.

Before you stop reading and call me a heretic, allow me to clarify. I'm not suggesting that God is female. God isn't female. God also isn't male. *God is God and isn't confined to gender. Period.* I am simply stating that the original names of *Yahweh* and *Ruach HaKodesh* include the masculine and feminine; therefore, we are made—male and female—in the image of God.

4. WHAT GIVES YOU JOY AND WHAT'S MOST CHALLENGING IN YOUR WORK?

For the better part of my life, I didn't believe I needed community because I was safer alone. I was so tired of being told I wasn't good enough, not smart enough, not pretty enough, not American enough, not Chinese enough, not Christian enough, not male enough. I was tired of being abandoned physically, mentally, and emotionally, which resulted in me pushing just about everyone away.

How many of us continue to choose that narrative? We've created a storyline that no one is *for* us. Everyone is *against* us. What an incredibly debilitating lie we have chosen to believe. Again, this is why *how* we view our triune God matters. If we believe God to be an angry God that will strike us down at any time and abandon us, we will not only treat others in that manner, but we will treat ourselves this way.

The most challenging part of my work is helping people see themselves the way God sees them—to realize their called purpose. However, this also provides me the most joy as it is an absolute privilege to share the truth of who God is as the God who is with us, who loves and anticipates us, who came to earth not as a warrior king, but as a homeless servant. A God who died so that we don't have to. A Savior who rose again to send our greatest Advocate who dwells among us right now. All this because God desires to be in proximity to us. More than anything, my passion is helping others view the triune God in a way that matters because this is how we will ultimately view each other and ourselves.

5. WHAT ADVICE DO YOU WISH SOMEONE HAD GIVEN YOU ABOUT YOUR CALL/MINISTRY?

More than three decades have passed since my mother asked me what I wanted to be when I grew up. I did not have the context, capacity, language, or understanding then, but today, I know I am called to love God and others and help usher humanity to the foot of his throne. If I could go back and whisper knowledge into the ears of my fourteen-year-old self, I would tell her this:

We are not created to be isolated.

We're not an accident stuck purposeless in this world.

We're not supposed to be all-knowing or the center of the universe.

Instead, we are created for community.

We are designed to trust and participate in fellowship with God and each other.

We are created to see and be seen.

To know and be known.

To love and be loved.

Beloved, do not make yourself smaller.

Take up all the space God gave you in this time so that you can be exactly who he created you to be . . . made in his Image.

I would also tell her that we would not be married to a pastor but would, instead, become one. God's plan for us is more extensive than anything we can imagine for ourselves.

Just keep following Christ—one step at a time.

8
CARE PASTOR
Katy Reed Hodges

Katy Reed Hodges is the Minister of Congregational Life at First Baptist Church Arlington, Texas. She has served FBCA for nine years and was ordained in 2017.

1. HOW DID YOU GET INTERESTED IN YOUR FIELD/MINISTRY?

It is fascinating to consider how I first got interested in the ministry of pastoral care because I began my ministry life, and worked for many years, in collegiate ministry. I cut my teeth in ministry working as an intern for a Baptist student ministry. I have also done residential campus ministry and church-based college ministry, including a six-year stint at my current church. When I sensed a call to something new (which we will discuss), I realized that what I had enjoyed and done well through each of those positions were the care and shepherding aspects of my role.

Most intensely, during my time at Truett Seminary I was a resident chaplain for two years, living and serving in two of Baylor's first-year residence halls. Through that, I had the opportunity to walk through crisis, grief, and hardship with many students and found it particularly meaningful. I also realized it seemed to be a good personality fit for me.

Over the twelve years total of college ministry, I came to learn that the age group of eighteen- to twenty-three-year-olds is a demographic ripe with pastoral care needs. The combination of learning independence, processing their family of origin, budding mental health issues, poor decision-making and many other factors made it a wonderful opportunity to intersect with a person's life when they greatly needed a pastor, and I found it very rewarding.

When the opportunity came for me as a thirty-five-year-old to apply for a pastoral care job, I was delighted that my church might consider me, a relatively young woman, to work closely with our pastor and serve the church in all areas of care and need. I felt that I could get to do the very thing I had been doing for the college students, but now do it for the whole church body. I am still very humbled and honored to serve in this role.

2. HOW DID YOU PROCESS YOUR CALL?

I have had a few distinct callings in my life. My initial call to ministry came while working at the Baptist student ministry at South Plains College in Levelland, Texas. At that time, the intern job was designed as a sort of discernment time for young men and women to work in full-time ministry for a year and discover what God might have for them moving forward. I took the job hoping that my time there would make my path clear, and it did. I was a high school education major in my undergraduate studies, and I was weighing if I ought to teach high school and be an involved churchwoman (God bless those who do walk this path), or if God was indeed calling me to full-time vocational ministry. I do not come from a family of ministers; they are all faithful church people. So, I took this time very seriously to consider what this might mean for my future—my potential family, my income, my work-life balance, etc. Through many ministry opportunities and several influential voices (almost all BSM leaders at the time), I discerned to the best of my ability that to be faithful to God in the next season, I should go to seminary, learn more, and prepare for vocational ministry. I remember feeling clearly that choosing to teach, for me, would have been the path of security and self-preservation, pitted against the choice to walk in faith to a new opportunity of seminary and vocational ministry. I don't know if I see things as dualistically now, but in that season, that is how I processed the move toward full-time ministry.

When I was nearing graduation at Truett, in my final semester, I sensed that God was preparing me for what was next through a series of experiences. I had loved working with college students and sensed that God continued to have that in store for me. Through Truett and my local church at the time, I had a much higher view of the church and its ability to be the Christ-chosen change agent that it could be in the world. I also had experiences at several different types of college campuses and realized I was better suited for a state school environment. And lastly, I had a deep conviction that I was a "moderate Baptist." So in my final semester of seminary I began praying something like, "Lord, I feel that you have equipped me to be a college minister at a moderate Baptist church next to a state school . . . but I don't think that job exists so I will go wherever you lead." Around April of my final semester my friend let me know about the college ministry job at First Baptist Church Arlington, which was planted firmly adjacent to the University of Texas at Arlington. At my first interview, I felt truly grateful that God had both put a calling in my heart and fulfilled it. I still feel grateful for those steps in that season.

Most recently, four years ago, I felt a similar stirring in my heart. My prayer went something like, "Lord, I feel like you're calling me to be an associate pastor at a smaller church." I felt a stirring to do what I was doing for the college ministry—care, shepherding, preaching, etc.—but for the whole church, and I was sure that I was going to need to leave to go find it in a smaller setting that would give me a chance. I was unaware that our pastoral care minister was about to leave and a door would be opened for me to not have to leave the church I loved, but to transition into a new season. Once again, I was humbled and so thankful that God provided meaningful work to match the calling he put within me.

3. WHO HELPED YOU DISCERN YOUR CALL?

In my initial call to ministry at the BSM in West Texas, my boss, Arlano Funderburk, was a crucial influence in my life. Arlano had lived through the SBC controversy and the fundamentalist takeover in the '80s and '90s and he wanted to make sure I was educated in the landscape through which I was walking. Having grown up Methodist, I really had no idea about any of it. Arlano gave me books to read and conferences to attend that helped begin to shape me into a young minister and helped me find my theological footing. Having a mentor like him at a pivotal age in my life gave me the rootedness I needed but did not yet have. Others in BSM did the same—a generation that is now all retired—and I am very grateful for their role in my life.

While at Truett Seminary, I felt extremely affirmed and seen in my formation as a young minister. I had ample opportunity to learn and grow and there are many people whom I should probably credit, but I will limit it to two.

I somehow ended up as the only female in Dr. Andy Arterbury's Gospels class. I didn't really notice because I had several friends there. Dr. Arterbury would make comments to me like, "Katy, when you are a pastor, how will you answer your congregants who ask . . . ?" or "When you pastor, how will you react when . . . ?" One day I stopped him after class and asked him what he was up to. He told me that if I were a man, I would have likely been affirmed fifty times in my giftedness that I should become a pastor, but because I was a woman he doubted that I had really considered it. He asked me to genuinely pray about it, so of course I did. I never have felt God calling me to the senior pastorate, but the affirmation in my pastoral giftedness meant so much to me that I clearly carry it with me today, ten years later.

Also, while I was at Truett I interned at my church, DaySpring Baptist Church, under the leadership of several of their pastors, including Tiffani Harris. Each of the pastors there was gifted in calling out and raising young leaders, and I remember one specific crucial moment for me. For a minute I debated applying for the college job at FBCA. I was weighing it against an associate role at a local campus ministry. It meant I wouldn't have to leave Waco (and my then-boyfriend, now-husband) and I wouldn't have to be the head leader; I could be the associate. I distinctly remember the affirmation of Tiffani saying, "You are ready to be the leader. You can do it." And that provided the push I needed to pursue the fullness of what God had for me. Tiffani spoke those small words of encouragement to me consistently for the three years I worked with her—and she still does to this day.

4. WHAT GIVES YOU JOY AND WHAT'S MOST CHALLENGING IN YOUR WORK?

I receive great joy from much of my position. The reality of my job is that I get to know people when their lives have taken a turn for the worse—through the death of a loved one, a financial need, a divorce, crisis, or other hardship. I don't relish any of that, but I do find satisfaction in mobilizing the church to show up when people need it the most. Like all ministers ought, I feel that my job is truly most important and without it, the people would perish. Who wants to go to a church where they don't handle a funeral with care, or show up to the hospital when you're sick? I feel that I do the very necessary foundational work that builds a healthy church, and that brings me joy. I feel that it is close to the heart of God, and fielding it well brings satisfaction.

I think the most challenging parts of my job are the nebulous boundaries and the nature of working on a large staff. Regarding boundaries, it is very difficult in this job to know when I've done enough and need to put it down for the day or the weekend. People are always hurting, and I believe what I do is very important. The work brings fatigue; it is always hanging over my head, and if I'm not careful to protect myself it can deplete my energy. This has only been magnified by having triplets in 2022. I have had some hard adjustments in the past few years, and it is certainly challenging to do all things well. Stating the obvious: Church work was easier before I had children.

I also work on a large staff, and it requires significant attention. In addition to care, I also sit on our staff's ministry lead team which directs and provides clarity to our ministers. I enjoy having a seat at the big table and find it very fulfilling, but it can take my attention away from my shepherding of the care ministries, which can make me feel distracted and pulled in many directions. Some weeks it is extremely challenging.

5. WHAT ADVICE DO YOU WISH SOMEONE HAD GIVEN YOU ABOUT YOUR CALL/MINISTRY?

I think I got terrific advice along the way, but there are some things you can only learn by doing. If I did have advice for a younger Katy, it would be to take better care of myself. Learn boundaries. Exercise. Don't feel guilty for taking time away. Stay close to the heart of God and obey what he says. Learn about your personality and act accordingly. Eugene Peterson describes ministry well with the title of his classic work *A Long Obedience in the Same Direction*—treat it as the long, faithful journey that it is.

9
CHURCH CURRICULUM WRITING

Grace Sangalang Ng

Grace Sangalang Ng is a member of The Two Cities team, a podcast about theology, culture, and discipleship.

1. HOW DID YOU GET INTERESTED IN YOUR FIELD/MINISTRY?

I have been involved in teaching God's Word from a young age, as the church I grew up in placed a high value on Scripture. I began teaching children about the Bible in middle school, and I am grateful for the love of God's Word that this church cultivated in me. In college, I studied English literature and realized how much I loved writing. I was also involved in Cru at UCLA, where God expanded my heart for missions and ministry. As I meditated on John 21:15–22, I sensed God's calling to feed his sheep, though I was not sure what that meant at the time or how God would orchestrate my path.

After college, I attended Talbot School of Theology at Biola University, where I studied Bible exposition and spiritual formation. I loved learning and wanted to continue studying, so I also pursued a doctorate in educational studies, researching how shame affects Asian American seminary students. As a second-generation Filipino American, I wanted to explore something that reflected the experiences of my community. Going through this doctoral program refined my research and writing skills and gave me an educational lens to help people learn more about God and grow deeper in their relationship with him.

After graduating with my doctorate, I moved to Ventura County, California, where Mission Church gave me the opportunity to write small group guides based on Sunday sermons. I felt this work brought together many of the things I loved—writing, teaching, and helping people grow in community. I have also had the opportunity to teach workshops on spiritual formation in various settings. While I did not have a clear-cut path for how God would use my gifts, he led me step by step to discover and develop the abilities he entrusted to me.

2. HOW DID YOU PROCESS YOUR CALL?

I processed my call through community by talking with mentors and friends about where I believed God was leading me. I also spent significant time in prayer and reflection, and seminary provided space to grow in self-awareness—both of my gifts and of my limitations and areas for growth.

When I began seminary, I planned to pursue vocational ministry on the mission field. I started at Talbot in Christian education, believing I would go into children's ministry. The church I grew up in had strict beliefs about where women could serve, and children's ministry was the only option open to me as a young woman who desired to pursue vocational ministry. I served as children's outreach director, but as I took courses at Talbot, I was increasingly drawn to Bible exposition and realized that children's ministry was not what I wanted to do long term. I changed my program to Bible exposition.

During my second year of seminary, I went through a traumatic experience that resurfaced many unprocessed emotions from my past. I felt overwhelmed and struggled with anxiety and depression. During that time, my spiritual director, therapist, and friends in the Institute of Spiritual Formation at Talbot walked with me and cared for me, even when I struggled to believe in God's love. Through their tangible expressions of his care—

holding space for my emotions and listening with patience—I found hope when I felt hopeless.

I also left my home church during this time and joined a supportive community where I could rest and recover from burnout. Experiencing unconditional love and care in that season compelled me to learn how to care deeply for others. I enrolled in a second master's program in spiritual formation, where I found healing and language to articulate my experiences. I wrote a thesis on how shame affects Asian Americans, which led me to continue the topic through doctoral studies in educational studies at Talbot. Over the next seven years, while working in Biola's finance department, I pursued this research.

After completing my doctorate, I accepted a government finance position in Ventura County, where my husband and I relocated. At Mission Church, I had the opportunity to apply my seminary training by writing message-based small group guides that facilitated conversation and relationship-building. Through the entire journey, I have remained open to whatever God has placed before me, even in unexpected ways.

3. WHO HELPED YOU DISCERN YOUR CALL?

Throughout my educational journey, many people affirmed my gifts in research and writing, and my desire to help others grow deeper in God's Word and in relationship with him and others. My professors at Talbot were especially encouraging. I am grateful for professors such as Dr. Ben Shin and Dr. Octavio Esqueda, who affirmed my abilities and gave me opportunities to teach in their classes. They supported me through the writing process and helped me persevere during graduate school. I am also thankful for my husband, Stanley, whom I met at Biola, who has encouraged me every step of the way.

My recent pastors and mentors, Jen Oakes and Jim Sheldon, at Mission Church, along with Tiana Spencer through the Intentionally Her Cohort, have continued to empower me with encouragement and opportunities to use my gifts. I have been blessed by examples of women serving in pastoral, preaching, teaching, and leadership roles. Their presence and influence have been a significant encouragement to me, helping me see my own gifts more clearly, to embrace them without shame, and to allow God to use them wherever he may lead.

4. WHAT GIVES YOU JOY AND WHAT'S MOST CHALLENGING IN YOUR WORK?

I love writing guides that help facilitate deeper discussion in groups. It is a joy to witness how God is at work in people's lives and to see them engage more deeply with his Word while building authentic community. It is especially meaningful to watch how providing safe spaces for vulnerability allows people to find freedom and healing from the shame they carry. While I had no idea how God would use all my education, writing group guides for small groups has been a sweet opportunity to draw on many aspects of my training and passions.

The most challenging part of my work has been overcoming my own insecurities and feelings of impostor syndrome. I have had to unlearn limitations imposed by others because of my gender, and I have needed to learn how to fully embrace the gifts God has given me. Living into my full identity as a beloved child of God has been a process, but through it he has shown me how to exercise my gifts with freedom—whether writing discussion guides, teaching a seminar, or preaching in a church or college setting.

5. WHAT ADVICE DO YOU WISH SOMEONE HAD GIVEN YOU ABOUT YOUR CALL/MINISTRY?

Calling is not a one-time event. It is a continual, moment-by-moment surrender to God, allowing him to lead us where he wants us in each season. Often he simply asks us to take the next step of obedience, even when we do not know where it will lead. As we obey, he prepares the way, provides what we need, and opens opportunities to use our gifts. Calling is not necessarily a career; it may look different in various stages of life. Ultimately, our primary calling is to live in our identity in Christ—

discovering who we are in him and how he has made us for his purposes. As we allow God to shape us, he will open doors for us to serve.

One of my favorite quotes on calling is from Cardinal John Henry Newman:

> God has created me to do Him some definite service. He has committed some work to me which He has not committed to another. I have my mission. I may never know it in this life, but I shall be told it in the next. I am a link in a chain, a bond of connection between people. He has not created me for naught. I shall do good; I shall do His work. I shall be an angel of peace, a preacher of truth in my own place, while not intending it if I do but keep His commandments. Therefore, I will trust Him, whatever I am, I can never be thrown away. If I am sick, my sickness may serve Him, in perplexity, my perplexity may serve Him. If I am in sorrow, my sorrow may serve Him. He does nothing in vain. He knows what He is about. He may take away my friends. He may throw me among strangers. He may make me feel desolate, make my spirits sink, hide my future from me. Still, He knows what He is about. (John Henry Newman, *Meditations on Christian Doctrine*)

10
COLLEGE PASTOR
Autumn Seacat

Autumn Seacat serves as college pastor at Vista Community Church in Temple, Texas.

1. HOW DID YOU GET INTERESTED IN YOUR FIELD/MINISTRY?

I am beyond grateful to serve as a college pastor in Temple, Texas. I love helping students in this pivotal time of life say yes to following Jesus. The work of meeting with students, preaching, mentoring, event planning, and more, is not only spiritually important, it's also a ton of fun. I love walking alongside students as they discern who it is God has made them to be. There is nothing in the world like helping a college student who thought they came to college to find themselves, find their Savior, Jesus. I am convinced that helping college students learn what it looks like to follow Jesus can have world-changing effects as we send them out into the "real world," and I am so grateful to God for inviting me into this ministry. Without a doubt, God led me and my husband here, but I had no idea this is where I would end up! I'm grateful God takes us along better paths than we can plan for ourselves.

2. HOW DID YOU PROCESS YOUR CALL?

When I accepted my call to ministry, I expected God to write in the clouds what he wanted me to do with my life. After becoming a Christian at age six and growing up in church, watching my dad pastor our church and my mom lead beside him, I believed God had something a little more glamorous in mind for me than the local church. For the record, I loved the church with my whole heart. My parents cultivated a healthy view of church, I was mentored by my children and youth pastors, and felt proud to invite my unchurched friends with me each week. Church was a place where I felt alive and full of joy.

My dad's work inspired me, but I couldn't just follow in his footsteps. I needed to change the world! My life needed to be spent doing work on the global scale: running a nonprofit, fighting against human trafficking, being a missionary, I don't know—changing the world somehow! So that is what I set out to do as a first-year student in college. I waited for a sign in the clouds from God that showed me what I should do with my life to be the world changer I knew he wanted me to be. Spoiler alert: I never saw anything in the clouds, so I just decided to get involved in church and pick a major.

During the first year, I was asked by a mentor, Ross Chandler, to be a youth intern over the summer at his church. I figured, "Why not?" and signed up for one of the best summers of my life. It was no international nonprofit, but to my surprise, it felt like important work.

I began to realize how changing the world could maybe look like helping to change a youth student's summer. It was an important summer in showing me that church ministry gave me this undeniable deep sense of joy and purpose. After that summer and some important moments on some mission trips to England and Germany, I began to feel a tug to really explore what a vocation in church ministry could look like.

I loved helping point others toward Jesus and his life-changing power. I began to feel an intense pull to the ministry of the church and upon reflection realized that this pull had been there all my life. I started to realize that maybe my desire to change the whole world said more about my desire to matter in the world than it did about my desire to really serve God and others. Through the "small" moments of ministry that no one else could see, no platform or global audience, I realized what it really meant for me to be part of "changing the world." World-changing ministry looks like a lot of people being obedient, loving God, and loving others around us wherever he has placed us.

3. WHO HELPED YOU DISCERN YOUR CALL?

While it took some years to help clarify what God's call on my life was, I often think about the moment I "surrendered" my life to ministry with such gratitude. As a first-year student in high school, I said yes to God during my youth group's Disciple Now weekend. The guest speaker invited those who felt called to ministry to walk forward during the invitation time. I resisted. No way was I going to bring attention to myself or be led by my emotions. But as I stood there, my heart began to burn in a way I have yet to experience since. I knew to my core that God wanted me to step forward and surrender my life and vocation to following him and loving others.

When I left the worship service that night, I called my parents to tell them what had happened. They responded in joy, saying, "We aren't surprised." They have been my biggest cheerleaders and have taught me to always say yes to the calling of God. I must pause and acknowledge that I am so blessed to have the parents, sisters, and mentors I have. They have always encouraged me to follow Christ wherever he leads—Bruce and Nancy Webb, my professors at Truett Seminary, my youth pastors growing up, Matt Poe and Ryan Chandler, Ross Chandler, Drew Humphrey, Sydney Pfleeger, Austin Fischer, and so on. I could go on about the many people in my life, many unnamed in this list, who have opened doors for me and encouraged me on my journey with Jesus. They have said yes to opening their lives and opportunities to me so that I can say yes to God.

I think about how different my life would be if my parents or mentors had responded differently to my calling. What if they had said "No"? Or, "We see your heart and desire to serve God, but let's channel that into marrying a pastor instead." Well, that would have been a shame because I would not have married my statistician husband, Graham Seacat, who has been the biggest blessing in my life, besides salvation, and my co-partner in ministry.

The land of "what ifs" is a dangerous place to spend too much time. However, over the years I have wondered, would I have said yes to Jesus if the people I loved had told me my desires to serve Jesus in the church pastorally were wrong? What if there is a dying world going to hell without the life-changing news that Jesus loves them and wants to save them and yet, there are women who have been told "No" to God's calling on their life to serve the church? What if they listened to that "No"? What if I had listened to that "No"?

This leads into the part of my calling story I wish I could leave out. It was in my sophomore year of college that I really became acquainted with the idea that there are Christians in the world that are passionate in their opposition to the idea of women in ministry. This was also the same year that I began to feel the pull toward vocational church ministry that I mentioned above. This was a new conversation to me, as I had grown up in a church that believes in and equips both men and women for gospel service and ministry. For the first time, however, I encountered some strong opposition to my desire to serve Jesus in the context of the local church.

Though I had even more people in my corner that taught me a scripturally sound defense of women leadership in the church, this opposition became a big stumbling block in my calling. In fact, it sent me into a dark spiral of doubt and confusion. Did I really hear Jesus correctly that I was called to church ministry? Am I really called by God? Well, as I wrestled through this call, I got a call on my phone from my college pastor. He said, "Autumn, would you like to be an intern for the college ministry?" And the rest became history. I spent the next five years on staff with my college ministry starting as a college intern and ending it as the associate college minister while I finished college and completed my master's from Truett Seminary. I truly believe that, as they say, if God calls you to it, he will see you through it.

4. WHAT GIVES YOU JOY AND WHAT'S MOST CHALLENGING IN YOUR WORK?

In my years of following Jesus, I have learned that he very rarely writes in the clouds what his plan and purpose for our entire lives are. Instead, Jesus just asks us to say yes to the opportunities he places before us, however small they might seem! These small yeses over a lifetime lead to a story that is more beautiful than we could imagine for ourselves. Though I have missed and said no to opportunities God has probably asked me to take advantage of, I have said some yeses to God that I am eternally thankful for. Here is a brief history of some of my yeses:

> My yes to being a youth intern led to a passion for church ministry. My yes in college to intern for my college ministry led to five years of life-changing ministry. This yes also led to me meeting my husband, Graham, over summer college ministry and saying a hearty yes to spending my life with him. My yes to Truett Seminary led to years of transformational theological education. My difficult yes to step away from college ministry during my last year of seminary led to a summer internship at Vista Community Church that taught me so much. My yes to working at First Baptist Church of Kaufman after seminary taught us that he really does guide our every step even when we don't understand it. That previous yes to the Vista internship led to another yes to now serve as the college pastor at Vista Community Church.

Graham and I have made the decision to say yes to God whenever and wherever. Each time we have said yes, we did not know how it would turn out, but we have grown confident that a life of saying yes to Jesus will always be better than a life of saying yes to our own desires and plans instead. We truly couldn't be more excited to be anywhere but at Vista Community Church. We believe in the importance of investing in college students and see how every step along the way has led to this amazing opportunity before us. Our desire above anything else is to stay obedient to Christ because he is worthy of it.

5. WHAT ADVICE DO YOU WISH SOMEONE HAD GIVEN YOU ABOUT YOUR CALL/MINISTRY?

The most important advice I have been given in ministry is to always make Jesus Christ the main thing. Let Jesus be the thing you are known for above anything else in your life. As a female in ministry, you might be drawn to fight the battle of women in ministry. It is a worthy endeavor to help others see why we need both men and women serving in the church, and to see the scriptural basis of such a claim. However, you and I have not been called to spread an agenda, but instead to spread the good news of Jesus Christ. Let Jesus be the loudest thing in your life—the loudest thing you preach and the loudest thing you hear. I wish, once again, that the women in ministry conversation was something I could skip over regarding calling, but it would be unfair to many women struggling with this and to my younger self to pretend it's a nonissue. But it should never be *the* issue. Jesus must always be the center of our lives, thoughts, and callings.

Ministry is not always easy, and imposter syndrome is real, but I am choosing to believe that God has placed me where I am for a reason. I never feel good enough for the tasks put before me, but again, my job is just to say yes. I love Jesus and I believe he is so worthy of our lives. I follow Christ imperfectly, but with an awareness that he is faithful to finish the work he has started in me.

11
CO-SENIOR PASTOR
Jeanette Salguero

Jeanette Salguero is co-senior pastor at the multicultural The Gathering in Orlando, FL. She is also founder and vice president of the National Latino Evangelical Coalition, and founder and executive director of the Carrion Hispanic Leadership Institute at Southeastern University (SEU).

1. HOW DID YOU GET INTERESTED IN YOUR FIELD/MINISTRY?

The journey to embracing one's calling is often deeply personal, and it is rooted in a blend of a person's life experiences, their understanding of who God is, and their sense of purpose. Such was my journey. My interest in becoming a pastor emerged from extremely difficult moments that afforded opportunities of growth and self-discovery.

The pull towards my calling began to take shape during my early childhood. Being raised in a home where the public image differed significantly from the private reality created unique challenges and complexities for me. The physical, emotional, and psychological dysfunction forged feelings of powerlessness, unworthiness, and distrust. Strangely, we were a faithful churchgoing family, and it was at the church where I met *Hermana* (Sister) Flores. As the seventy-two-year-old children's director, she carefully cultivated in me a love for God, his word, and his church. During Sunday school she would ask me to do treasure hunts of verses in the Bible that affirmed my identity in God and his love for me. I felt safe, loved, and affirmed by the church.

Through this community, my faith deepened, and I found genuine connection. The instability at home could not pierce the church walls, so I found ways to spend a lot of time there. I volunteered for everything possible. If Sister Flores swept the church patio, I offered to carry the dustpan. If Sister Flores went to pray, I happily volunteered to carry the kneeling pillow. Her genuine love and care were invaluable in my life. Her love for Jesus and others ignited in me a determination to exude the same love towards others. And at age nine I promised God that I would serve him the rest of my days loving and helping others just as *Hermana* Flores did.

I shared the promise I made to God with Sister Flores. Her response changed my life forever: "Jeanette, you are set apart to shepherd people and help them know that they are loved." She then asked me to memorize Romans 8:28 and to carry it in my heart forever: "And we know that in all things God works for the good of those who love him, who have been called according to his purpose" (NIV). At that moment I had no idea that this verse would be foundational to my ministerial longevity. The promise in this verse has given me hope in adversity. It has motivated me to persevere in my calling, and it has instilled in me a fresh perspective on challenges—that no matter what happens, God is on his throne, and I know how the last chapter of my life ends—I win!

God's word for me is not just words on paper. I believe that it is God's voice to humanity. As such, I approach it with an open heart, giving it room to transform me. I believe Hebrews 4:12, "For the word of God is alive and active. Sharper than any double-edged sword, it penetrates even to dividing soul and spirit, joints and marrow; it judges the thoughts and attitudes of the heart" (NIV). Without the word, our interest in ministry will become a personal endeavor void of the essential fuel that gives it sustainability.

2. HOW DID YOU PROCESS YOUR CALL?

The pillars that nudged me towards processing my pastoral calling were the community of saints and the consistent embrace of spiritual disciplines. The church community offered spiritual leaders and friends that encouraged me and offered support. My pastor at the time paved the way for hands-on experience and launched me to teach children. As I grew in wisdom and maturity, I transitioned to preaching at youth services. My hermeneutical and homiletical skills were being sharpened. But before placing me on a Sunday pulpit, the pastor wisely transitioned me to lead community outreach programs.

These opportunities gave me practical experience but also gave me insight into how to deal with people and how to love them—even those that were difficult. This process took time. In fact, from the moment I made the promise at age nine to when I was anointed to lead a congregation—twenty-two years had passed. This was not a microwave development. It was a lengthy process by which the Father slowly and continuously called me unto himself, and the church was pivotal in this. The church provided a unique and enriching environment that helped me process my calling. It was the ground that helped me develop a heart for service. One thing is for sure: A minister in training that is not connected to a local church community is like a fledgling swimmer without a pool.

There is no way one can speak life into a person without first being in relationship with them. I love and believe in the church despite all its vicissitudes. Yes, humanity lurks inside its walls and many times it must be called to order. But Jesus bought it with his own blood, and it behooves anyone processing their call to love the church and keep watch over it (Acts 20:28, NIV).

Time in prayer, meditation, reflection, scripture reading, study, worship, and fasting were also crucial to how I processed my call. These spiritual disciplines were the underpinning of character formation. They still are. You see, there is absolutely no way that one can be in God's presence and not change. It was in prayer and meditation that the initial spark of my calling turned into a burning conviction. The intentional practice of being in God's presence not only fostered a spiritual awakening but it also gave me a deeper understanding of myself. It was in God's presence where the effects of my upbringing lost their power. It was these moments that gave me the opportunity to wrestle with the ugly parts of my heart and walk towards inner peace. It is impossible to process one's call without spending time with the one who invites you to the call.

3. WHO HELPED YOU DISCERN YOUR CALL?

Discerning God's specific purpose for my life involved a combination of serving in different capacities at my local church, seeking God, and devouring resources that offered biblically centered advice. But there were two people that I intentionally sought out to pray with me and be a sounding board because of their spiritual maturity. Raquel was a lead pastor. John was my therapist. I chose them because I needed impartial voices outside of my immediate circle to both encourage and challenge me.

Raquel was a powerful pastor with vast experience in shepherding people and she gladly agreed to be my spiritual mentor. She was ahead of me in life and ministry. Her words of wisdom helped me grow in faith and character. She modeled Christlike behavior and encouraged me to grow in love, humility, and patience. Raquel eventually became my mother-in-law and is still today one of my biggest cheerleaders and a guiding voice in my life.

John was a retired pastor who was also a therapist. He was a gift from God who helped me rebuild that which my upbringing tried to destroy. John taught me how to love myself and offered valuable tools to navigate different challenges in life. Intellectually, I was ready to launch. Emotionally, I had a lot of growing up to do. And so, with the guidance of the Holy Spirit, John gently tilled the ground of my heart to unearth potential ministerial stumbling blocks. While this *tilling* is an iterative process for me (it should be for all of us), the initial basic work was necessary because authentic leadership is rooted in personal healing and emotional health. Therapy or some form of counseling offers many benefits that help one walk into their vocation with clarity and well-being.

From my church to Sister Flores to Raquel to John, one thing is for sure: Discerning a call is a communal process.

4. WHAT GIVES YOU JOY AND WHAT'S MOST CHALLENGING IN YOUR WORK?

Doing the will of God brings me great joy. In his infinite mercy, he recruited me! Co-laboring with him ushering in his shalom fulfills me. The fact that I get to team up with him blows my mind.

Seeing the impact of transformed lives also gives me joy. The opportunity to leave a legacy of a holistic gospel that outlives me fuels me. Mother Teresa stated it perfectly: "Give the world the best you have, and it may never be enough. But give the best you've got anyway." And so the call to pastoring, while at times physically and emotionally exhausting, is made worth it in witnessing the transformation in people's lives.

One of the challenging areas of the calling is being misunderstood and mislabeled. Mischaracterization can be emotionally and spiritually depleting. Especially when, for the most part, pastors invest deeply in the ministry. And so, if one is not careful, mislabeling can feel personal. As such, my immunization is prayer and meditation on scripture. Maintaining a strong prayerful life and staying in his word reminds me of the promise I made forty-two years ago. These disciplines keep me grounded and centered on the one who called me rather than the challenges. I can't control all the narratives, but prayer and meditation keep me integrated. "Watch and pray so that you will not fall into temptation. The spirit is willing, but the flesh is weak" (Matthew 26:41, NIV).

5. WHAT ADVICE DO YOU WISH SOMEONE HAD GIVEN YOU ABOUT YOUR CALL/MINISTRY?

Remember, it's a marathon, not a sprint! That is the advice that I wish someone had shared with me about ministry early on. I would have avoided one too many anxious episodes. But not understanding the marathonic element of ministry is, I believe, a major ailment in twenty-first-century ministries. I see too many people launching immediately after the initial tug of the call and running to establish the biggest and greatest next thing—yielding their *being* under the weight of *doing*. Then we witness the personal atrocities that bring a bad name to the gospel. And as a doer, an overachiever, and an impatient person (weaknesses that I must take to the cross daily), I understand the gruesome fight with dissatisfaction and ministerial insatiability. One sees the projects of others growing fast and if one is not careful, one can become a victim of hurriedness and competition. Then, rather than achieving genuine growth, one swells. Swelling may look like growth, but swelling in the body leads to tissues becoming stiff and highly susceptible to injury.

The preparation for the pastorate is lengthy. In fact, it never ends. The internal work is incessant. Planting healthy churches and launching sustainable ministries takes time. Therefore, I remind myself of Paul's advice, "Brothers and sisters, I do not consider myself yet to have taken hold of it. But one thing I do: Forgetting what is behind and straining toward what is ahead, I press on toward the goal to win the prize for which God has called me heavenward in Christ Jesus" (Philippians 3:13–14, NIV).

12
SENIOR PASTOR
Mandy Smith

Mandy Smith is the pastor of St Lucia Uniting Church in Brisbane, Australia. Her latest book is *Confessions of an Amateur Saint: The Christian Leader's Journey from Self-Sufficiency to Reliance on God.*

1. HOW DID YOU GET INTERESTED IN YOUR FIELD/MINISTRY?

I grew up in an Australian Churches of Christ congregation where we didn't know women's ordination was an issue. Maybe it was just a practical matter—with limited resources and few leaders, many churches in Australia need all the help they can get. In this context, ministry was not primarily about power or job titles but about servanthood, which, of course, everyone, regardless of gender, is called to. I knew that choosing to follow Jesus meant giving your whole life, so at eleven, when, at a girls' camp, I gave my life to God, I thought it might mean becoming a missionary like the woman who baptized me. But that seemed like a far-off, grown-up thing so I set about just learning to listen to God in my ordinary little life.

At sixteen I met Jamie, a zealous young man, who, at twenty, was more serious about Bible study than anyone I'd ever met. He had a plan to study the Bible in America one day and eventually to teach at a seminary. I liked the idea of supporting a husband in his ministry as seminary professor (which is a wonderful calling in which I have served for twenty-five years but not the only calling God had for me).

Before we knew it, we were married and in the United States for Bible college. But because we hadn't known women's ordination was an issue, we found ourselves studying at a Restoration Movement college in the Midwest that was known for its strong stance against women in leadership. Now I was asked to name my call in terms of job titles. If it was "children's director" or "women's ministry leader" that was okay. But was it a sin if the title was "pastor"? All it really felt like at the time was "joyful, obedient daughter of God."

2. HOW DID YOU PROCESS YOUR CALL?

At a Midwestern Bible college in the '90s, women's leadership was perceived by professors as a threat to orthodoxy (I took the "Feminism" class, which was part of a series of classes that included "Cults" and "The Occult"). Among students the question of women's roles fueled daily heated conversations. And so, like my classmates, I read all the books and engaged in all the debates, but debates could not remain objective for long as I felt my future being batted around the room. Alongside Christian commentaries I was reading secular feminism and took on its indignation—it's my right to do this work! But I soon had to decide: Would I choose to be understood and welcomed outside of the church or misunderstood and maligned among Christians? Would I define myself first as a woman or first as a Christian? I had to choose the latter. But it meant remaining in many painful places.

I felt caught between the Bible and a hard place. The God in the Bible and the church seemed to say I couldn't lead or teach. On the other hand, the God in my heart just said, "Follow me" with no caveats. My choice seemed to be, set aside your call to ministry so you can be a faithful Christian or set aside your faith so you can be a complete woman. Although I ached for resolution I refused to embrace a false choice. So I watched and waited and wrestled with God.

Thankfully, I wasn't alone. When it was time to choose a word to study in Greek class Jamie chose *hesuchia* (quiet or silent) from 1 Timothy 2:11–12. He was excited to discover that it did not simply mean auditory silence but also inner peace. But I did not have inner peace. And it was because of this very passage. Still, something in my young heart wanted to trust that in God all things hold together. And so, although I was far from peaceful, I chose to believe that God himself is harmony itself—God in the Bible, God in the church, God in my heart is all one God. I chose to believe I was not in conflict with God, that God was not in conflict within himself. The problem was my limited understanding.

And so for years Jamie and I waited together in all that could not be resolved, searching history and language and prayer for every sign of what this meant for me and my calling. While God eventually brought resolution to our questions, I see now the ironic grace: God used this very tension about leadership to prepare me for leadership. Learning this posture of peace and this "hermeneutic of *hesuchia*" prepared me for ministry more than the quick answers I would have preferred.

It would be some years before God opened the doors for me to do anything that looked like a professional ministry career. The hermeneutic of *hesuchia* served me during the fourteen years after Bible college when I worked as an administrator while Jamie completed his PhD, then as a stay-at-home mom and freelance writer. By now I had done the work of discerning my interpretation of Scripture about women's roles, but when I finally stepped into church leadership there were entirely new levels of discernment to engage.

When the congregation chose me to be their first female lead pastor (and the first female lead pastor in their movement of six thousand congregations) none of us—me included—had any idea what it might mean. Having never taken a preaching class (girls took "Public Speaking"), I had to learn my own cadence of preaching (it took months to realize my throat was sore after preaching because I was inadvertently lowering my voice). As I made decisions, cast vision, and led staff, we all had to navigate cultural baggage and shape new categories: What is a feminine pastoral leader if not "counselor" or "boss-lady" or "mom"? There were many fine lines to walk—authoritative but not bossy, feminine but not too feminine, approachable but not too emotional, collaborative but not a pushover.

I don't claim to have walked any of those fine lines perfectly. I trust that the times we all learned the hard way were part of the grace he wanted to show to us. In failure I choose not to heed the voices of those who have said, "See, that's proof you're not called to this!"

3. WHO HELPED YOU DISCERN YOUR CALL?

It's been hard to even discern who to trust in my discernment of call. As a deeply communal person who wants to submit herself to God's speaking through the church, this discernment has been excruciating and isolating: Where is the church speaking on God's behalf and where is it not? When church leaders have told me my sense of call is a lie from the devil, whom do I believe? When what feels like the Spirit in me is contradicted by those in Christian authority over me, whose voice do I heed?

So, I'm thankful that in it all God has provided friends and champions. I'm blessed to have a husband who grew up in grass-roots church plants founded by his Spirit-led mum and who has, for thirty-five years, made sacrifices to make my work possible. And I'm grateful for Troy, who was my pastor for five years before I began as his associate pastor. In dark moments, Troy quoted Howard Thurman: "Don't ask what the world needs. Ask what makes you come alive and go do it. Because what the world needs is people who have come alive." And in my first role as senior pastor, I was blessed to have Anthony as my associate, who embraced the discomfort of being led in a way he'd never been led before. As much as I have "ghosts" who haunt me with fearful, negative stories, God has provided real humans who tell a different story, like my colleague Winn, who often stops me in the middle of defending an idea to say, "Mandy, I trust you"—the best kind of interruption I know.

4. WHAT GIVES YOU JOY AND WHAT'S MOST CHALLENGING IN YOUR WORK?

In a time when the church is in upheaval, we can rarely know the outcomes of our work. I want to see lives changed, hearts healed, and communities brought into peace with God and one another. I rarely see it as much as I want. Every day I wake with an awareness of the challenges the day holds. Every day I'm tempted to just fix, control, and understand in my own strength. I just want to know outcomes, to see miracles, and to feel successful.

But the joy of this whole story I've been telling is that God is with us in every unresolved thing. Something of that hermeneutic of *hesuchia* remains with me still, reminding me that although so much seems to be in conflict in me, the church, and the world, there is a God who is one, who holds all things together, who is making all things new. I can't fully see it. But I choose to trust that the problem is not in God but in my limited understanding. It's not a comfortable way to live each day. But I'm getting used to the discomfort. And from that place I invite others to join me, trusting one day at a time that God is not far off, that he wrestles with us in all the unresolved things, that the story isn't finished but we know the ending.

5. WHAT ADVICE DO YOU WISH SOMEONE HAD GIVEN YOU ABOUT YOUR CALL/MINISTRY?

I wish that a long time ago someone had said these words to me so let me end by saying them to you, brothers and sisters:

> You are called to empty and to give yourself away—Jesus asks us to give our time, energy, and gifts for the sake of others. And at the same time, Jesus did not answer every question, did not entrust himself to everyone. He knew when to wipe the dust off his feet, when to keep his pearls to himself.

Women are often socialized to defer so much that they lose sense of their own selves. Such sacrifice feels Christian, but Jesus's emptying did not make him nobody but such a somebody! He was his true self and chose to use his agency to serve the needs of others.

As the Western church is becoming increasingly aware and appropriately cautious of abuses of power, it's common to hear warnings like, "Don't seek the limelight. Don't speak up." I've heard people say, "We don't do leadership anymore"—an overcorrection from abusive leadership. The answer to abusive authority is not to set aside authority but to embrace Christlike authority—the kind that comes from obedience to the Father.

Those who (due to gender, personality, or circumstance) are driven towards leadership may need to exercise caution, to step back, to listen more. They may need to be wary of ego. And at the same time, there are others who (due to gender, personality, or circumstance) are more likely to recede. These more deferential folks may need to heed the lessons of the prophets who, when called by God, shrunk back, asking, "Who am I?" In response, God never convinced them to lead based on their own capacity but drew their eyes to the source of their call—himself. For folks who defer, the refusal to step into calling may look like humility, but it may be disobedience.

Underuse of power is also power abuse.

To every question about what it means both to be fully yourself and to fully live out your calling, let me say this final word: The things that seem to disqualify you are opportunities for God to show you who he is. The parts of you that feel shameful are places God wants to heal so you have real good news to share. The weak places in you are the places God can best reveal his strength.

13
WOMEN'S MINISTRY
Emily Kelly

Emily Kelly serves as women's minister at Highland Baptist Church in Waco, Texas, and is a contract writer for Yarrow, an imprint of nonprofit publisher Precept.

1. HOW DID YOU GET INTERESTED IN YOUR FIELD/MINISTRY?

As I consider the roots of my interest in women's ministry, I can't ignore the formative years of my childhood. My parents had rich relationships with Christ. They each had a prayer life and devotion to the scriptures that shaped my own. Outside our home they were gifted vocational ministers, and were just as devoted to ministry inside the home. Depending on their season of life, they served as evangelists, teachers, and shepherds in both local church and parachurch ministries. Mom and Dad would be the first to tell you that they weren't perfect. But anyone who knew them would agree that they were captivated by Jesus and deeply loved people. Their private lives matched their public lives, and this coherence softened my young heart towards the gospel's credibility.

In the fall of 1992, I entered another spiritual incubator for my heart: my kindergarten class at a small private school. Our teacher,

Mrs. Colquitt, was gracious and poised. From my five-year-old perspective, everything she said and did exuded safety and welcome. Our teacher's aide, Mrs. Weatherly, kept a smile on her face. As with most kindergarten teachers, we never doubted if they were happy to see us. One morning I sat cross-legged in the back of our classroom. Even now I can vividly picture the primary colors on the walls and feel the woven color-block rug beneath my fingers. Mrs. Colquitt took a few minutes to share with us that every person was created to have a relationship with God. But we have all been born in sin, separated from our Creator.

The good news is that through Jesus's death and resurrection, God did everything needed to bring us back to himself. All that is needed from us is to trust in Jesus's work instead of our own and to let him be in charge of our lives. Although I'd heard this message before, the Spirit moved in my heart that day. I knew I needed Jesus and asked Mrs. Weatherly to pray with me. At the time I could only describe it as a personal invitation for me from Jesus himself to follow him.

I will never forget the joy and welcome I sensed from him towards me, even as a young child. I started this chapter on women's ministry with my salvation experience for two reasons. First, apart from the compassion and grace of God towards me in Christ, I would not be able to rightly love those I serve in ministry. Secondly, my salvation story is one example of how God uses women to call people to himself. My earliest memory of someone outside my home speaking truth to my heart is these two women. The context was not a pew or a revival tent; it was a simple kindergarten classroom. But from a kingdom perspective, it was a prime opportunity for two women to act as ministers of reconciliation in their God-given sphere of influence. Their love for Christ and for their students also planted a seed of faith in my heart about every woman who follows him: God does mighty things when women who follow Christ are equipped and released to fulfill their ministries. As a vocational women's minister now, my aim is to equip such women for this purpose, no matter their vocation or sphere of influence.

2. HOW DID YOU PROCESS YOUR CALL?

The summer before my first year of high school I attended a ten-day camp in Chattanooga, Tennessee, at the home of Precept Ministries. We studied the book of Romans inductively, learning to study the Bible for ourselves. God used this season to instill in me a love for his word as a means of knowing him rightly and personally. From there, I was blessed to be discipled by older women throughout high school and college. Then as opportunities arose, I began to disciple younger women myself. My heart developed the desire to help other women understand the Bible as the primary way that God reveals himself to them directly, accurately, and personally.

During my senior year of undergrad at the University of Georgia I spent a semester at the Focus Leadership Institute in Colorado. While there, I worked for a ministry that traveled to high schools to teach students a biblical worldview. Through this experience, I sensed a clear call from the Lord to pursue vocational ministry with the same group of people, in the same place, for a long period of time. One of the chaplains who worked for the Fellowship of Christian Athletes (FCA) at UGA called and offered me a job. I returned and worked for FCA at UGA for two and a half years until joining the staff of my local church full-time in college ministry. I worked with this church for five years, creating and implementing a discipleship ministry for the college women at the church.

In fall 2015, our family moved from Athens, Georgia, to Waco, Texas, for my husband's new job at Baylor University. At the time, the thought of serving a population other than college students had never crossed my mind. But not long after joining our new local church, Highland, volunteer needs arose in the adults' ministry. I began to serve as a member whenever a need arose that matched my availability. I tried service opportunities even if they weren't my "first choice." I began to develop relationships with women in the congregation, and stepped into opportunities to disciple, administrate, and teach, just as I had with college ministry in previous years. Staff and lay leaders gave me the priceless gift of mentorship, offering training, correction, encouragement, and so much grace. To say that Highland equipped, trusted, and empowered me as a woman in ministry would be an understatement. Then in 2019 I joined the staff team as the groups coordinator, helping members connect to small groups.

3. WHO HELPED YOU DISCERN YOUR CALL?

Throughout my life I've had mentors, friends, church leadership, and a supportive husband who have helped me discern how God has asked me to function in my call as a disciple maker. While working as groups coordinator, I and others at Highland began to see the opportunity for a more structured, women-specific ministry. As of 2020, the established avenues of women's ministry were a Bible study, a biannual women's retreat, and a ministry to moms of preschoolers. During the pandemic the church was growing rapidly, both numerically and in spiritual hunger. There was an increasing felt need among women, and they were tracing felt needs to their deepest spiritual need for God. Not only was there a growing sense of need among women, but there was also great potential to meet the need. In my staff and volunteer roles, I got to know countless Christlike, gifted women. They were diverse in demographics and backgrounds, with a variety of gifts and strengths. Highland had ministry needs and we had women to meet that need. All that was missing was a system to equip and connect these women to the ministry opportunities. It soon became clear to church leadership that God was leading Highland to pursue a new season of women's ministry. After several months of prayer, conversations, and conviction, I was offered and accepted the role of women's minister and began in January 2021.

4. WHAT GIVES YOU JOY AND WHAT'S MOST CHALLENGING IN YOUR WORK?

While there are many challenges in women's ministry, the greatest for me is my own pride and ego. I often feel a strong, fleshly sense of entitlement to the praise of people. It's tempting to take credit for things that go well and to shift the blame when things go wrong. Every day presents at least one opportunity to die to these desires. I've learned (often the hard way!) that Christlike leaders want to please the one who enlisted them (2 Timothy 2), give away credit when ministry succeeds, and accept full responsibility when ministry goes awry. Learning to deny myself, take up my cross, and follow Jesus has often taken these forms in women's ministry.

My greatest joy in women's ministry has been to equip the women of Highland in their ministries. When I started this job, I felt underqualified. And by the world's standards, I was underqualified! But I wasn't alone. For more than one hundred years, God has provided Highland with wise, gifted women who have actively ministered in "unpaid" capacities. I was hired as the church's first full-time women's minister, but I am not the first or only minister to women in the four-thousand-member congregation. If any ministry leader were to run as though the ministry relied solely on her, it would fail miserably.

During my first few months in the role, I met with a small vision team to discern the future of women's ministry at Highland. As we prayed and brainstormed, we kept returning to the words of the apostle Paul in Ephesians 4:11–13: "And [Christ] gave the apostles, the prophets, the evangelists, the shepherds and teachers, to equip the saints for the work of ministry, for building up the body of Christ" (ESV). Notice that it is the saints—all believers in Christ—who are to be equipped for ministry. The Greek word translated "equip" could also mean "complete furnishing (objectively):—perfecting" (*Strong's Concordance*, G2677). The Lord developed in me a conviction that my role as women's minister was to help give the women of Highland what they needed to step into their personal ministries—be that within the women's ministry or elsewhere!

We named the ministry "Highland Women" and created a mission statement to guide and protect its direction: Highland Women exists to provide intentional environments where women can walk together as disciples of Jesus. Our desire is to equip women to know God, to grow in Christ together, and to make disciples in our spheres of influence (Ephesians 4:11–16, Colossians 1:28–29). We knew it was not sustainable for Highland to have the same few women doing all the teaching, leading, and discipling. This was also true for soul care, caring for single moms, sharing the gospel, planning events, and more. And so, we formed five separate areas of ministry within Highland Women: women's Bible study, women's discipleship, women's soul care, the little years, and special events. We developed purpose statements for each area, ensuring that they each met a specific need while still aligning with the broader vision of Highland Women to make disciples. Each of the five ministry areas was then entrusted to its own gifted, trusted ministry team to steward and lead.

Since 2021, my role has become primarily to cast vision, recruit, develop, provide for, and partner with those teams to fulfill their ministries. Then those teams go and do the same for their volunteers. Because these gifted lay leaders share the vision of furnishing others for ministry, Highland Women has expanded to include over 250 volunteers and leaders: Bible study facilitators, soul care providers, mentor moms, teachers, disciplers, event coordinators, welcome teams, prayer warriors, evangelists, and more. In recent months the Spirit has led our leaders to pursue more opportunities for local evangelism and missions. We have no doubt that God will use the women of Highland to reach the world with the hope of Christ.

5. WHAT ADVICE DO YOU WISH SOMEONE HAD GIVEN YOU ABOUT YOUR CALL/MINISTRY?

One of my favorite things to repeat to our leaders and volunteers is, "Every woman who follows Christ is a minister." I wish someone had told me this years ago, but I'm grateful the Lord gave me this conviction before starting in this specific role. A woman who follows Christ might have a personal ministry that's vocational or volunteer, formal or informal. It might take place in the local church or outside of it. But every woman who follows Christ has a profound role to play in his kingdom. The women of Highland are some of the strongest, most gracious, and generous ministers I know. It is an honor to help equip them to fulfill their callings.

14

WORSHIP MINISTRY

Jessica Lackey

Jessica Lackey is the Associate Gathering Minister of Worship at Highland Baptist Church in Waco, Texas. She also serves at a variety of ministries, including Breakaway Ministries at Texas A&M and The Worship Initiative.

1. HOW DID YOU GET INTERESTED IN YOUR FIELD/MINISTRY?

There is a frame on my desk at the church that is home to a tiny, perforated piece of paper from 2009. Creased, smudged, and covered in my ninth-grade handwriting, it holds details such as what church I was from, who my youth pastor was, and to my continued embarrassment, it immortalizes my middle school email address: justletmerock04@gmail.com. Fourteen-year-old Jessica was listening to a *lot* of Evanescence, Paramore, and My Epic.

At the bottom of the form are three different checkbox prompts: the first to commit one's life to Jesus, the second to continue in obedience with baptism. It is next to the third prompt that I placed a check mark: "I am committing to serve God in ministry." I hardly remember the youth conference that I was at. I have no recollection of the speaker or where I was, and at the time I certainly had no idea what all such a commitment would mean. Yet throughout the years I have held onto that tiny slip of paper as an Ebenezer, a reminder that "thus far the Lord has helped" through a journey that has been both laced in joy and fraught with frustration.

To begin my story of the call to a life of service to the church, I must first begin with the story of the call of Jesus on my life to himself. There is hardly a piece of my being that has not been shaped, diapered, disciplined, taught, or loved by the church. As the only child of a Southern Baptist pastor in Mississippi, the entirety of my life has been surrounded by the people of God and the service given unto them. My earliest memories are of green sanctuary carpet meeting dark wooden pews with deep red cushions, running to the organist during the greeting part of the service to grab a peppermint, excitedly exchanging my Awana Bucks for animal-shaped erasers, or, if I was alone on a weekday that my dad was working on sermon prep, pushing the wheelchairs to the top of the slanted breezeway and rolling down in glee (I most certainly was told not to do that, but this was pre-sanctification!). The first thirteen years of my life were marked by career ministry much more than discipleship to Jesus.

My eighth-grade year began a reckoning of faith. Like so many tragic stories and church statistics, my family fell into disrepair when it was brought to light that my father had been having an ongoing affair with a church member. After a year of trying and failing at restoration, my parents divorced, and my mother and I crossed state lines to the Northshore of New Orleans. Confused, battered, and afraid, I was forced to sift through the truth and lies of both my father and the faith that he so boldly professed with his mouth but betrayed with his life.

To express the journey of redemption that the Lord brought in the aftershock of my parents' divorce would be a book unto itself. Instead, I will summarize by saying that Jesus would not let me go. One of my favorite songs is "Mystery" by Charlie Hall. It very simply declares, "Sweet Jesus Christ, my sanity. Sweet Jesus Christ, my clarity." Jesus has been my only sanity and clarity in a life coated in turmoil. I resonate deeply with the words of Peter when Jesus asks him in John 6 if he wants to jump ship: "Lord, to whom will we go? You have the words of eternal life. We have come to believe and know that you are the Holy One of God" (John 6:68–69, CSB).

2. HOW DID YOU PROCESS YOUR CALL?

The call to vocational ministry in my life has continued to be so intricately woven with the call to Jesus that I hardly know where one ends and the other begins. It reminds me of yet another conversation between Peter and Jesus on the beach after Jesus's resurrection: "'Simon, son of John, do you love me?' 'Yes, Lord,' he said to him, 'you know that I love you.' 'Shepherd my sheep,' he told him" (John 21:16, CSB). Just around the time that I was surrendering my life to love and follow Jesus, I felt his beckoning to shepherd his sheep as well. Early on, however, I had no discerning thought as to what exactly that meant. I craved guidance. I mentioned briefly to a student leader that I was feeling the tug to vocational ministry and was met with a passive comment that I'm still unraveling to this day: "You must not know what the voice of God sounds like, because God wouldn't call you to something that you aren't allowed to do as a woman."

Stunned and yet entirely trusting, I took his words to heart. Convincing myself that I had merely imagined what Eugene Peterson called a "burning in my bones," I decided that counseling was the next best thing to vocational ministry. I headed off to Houston Baptist University a few years later to pursue a degree in psychology, but the burning I felt persisted quietly. This youth leader's comment hindered my ability to process my call for *years*. It took the discerning and loving guidance of trusted pastors and mentors to give me the confidence to process the call for myself.

3. WHO HELPED YOU DISCERN YOUR CALL?

In my time in student ministry, I was a part of my student worship band. My musical knowledge was limited, but in high school Jessica so desperately wanted to be Hayley Williams. A couple of years in my youth band gave me just enough experience to be moderately helpful when I got to college, and Joel, the worship pastor at the church I was a part of, asked me to join for the middle school retreat to lead a few songs around the campfire. I cannot begin to express how pivotal that trip was. The magnitude was subtle. There was no beacon of light from heaven that came down to declare, "This is where I have you. Lead my people in worship of me." Rather, the shift came with the beginning of discipleship. Joel took me under his wing. What began with singing a few songs around a campfire became an invitation to lead alongside him on Sunday mornings, to spend time with his wife and children, to pop up to the church on a weekday to learn about Planning Center, and to have long conversations about the importance of song for the Body.

For four years, Joel invested in me. With every passing week, I learned both the theology and the logistics of worship ministry. He embodied the "I do, we do, you do" model of discipleship, bringing me alongside as he prayerfully planned worship sets, faithfully loved a team, graciously fielded "kind regards" from church members, and humbly led our local body in worship of the triune God. After a couple of years, he handed off more and more responsibility to me. When I think back to just how awkward and terrible some of those first nights of worship were, I am abundantly grateful for the patience of Joel. He gave me space to fumble around, to ask questions, to fail, to be arrogant and then humbled, and to grow from my mistakes.

As my time in college ended, I began to panic. While I held counselors in high esteem with gratitude, I was miserable at the thought of continuing to grad school for something that I was only mildly interested in. Those words spoken to me in high school were still rattling me. With deep fear welling within me despite his continued encouragement, I timidly mentioned to Joel one day that I didn't want to do counseling, and that maybe Jesus was calling me to serve his church in the same way Joel did.

"Oh, was that not already clear? I thought you were already certain of this. Jessica, Jesus has absolutely gifted and called you to this."

Jesus says in John 10:27 (CSB), "My sheep hear my voice, I know them, and they follow me." After six or so years of doubting, I finally began to trust that I did indeed know my Shepherd's voice. To this day, I am passionate about calling out and affirming the God-given gifts in others because I know that the shouting of the wolves can drown out the still small voice.

Following this encouraging affirmation from both Joel and several other trusted mentors, I followed their advice to continue to flesh out the calling in the safety and direction of seminary. "Safety" feels a bit humorous to say now, because seminary was easily the hardest thing I've ever met. The absolute shakedown of all you have ever been taught about Jesus, down to the foundation to then be built back up, is a brutal process. Not everyone survives it. I watched friend after friend either drop out of seminary, drop out of ministry, or leave the faith entirely. The grace of God alone sustained me, and four years later I graduated from Truett with my master of divinity.

After eight years of Disciple Now weekends, summer camps, worship nights, and Sunday morning rhythms, I was thoroughly convinced that my graduation would mark the beginning of "actual" vocational ministry. Two weeks shy of graduation and three weeks shy of marriage, I found myself in the later rounds of a job interview to serve on staff for a ministry to college students that I had been leading worship with for years. Jesus had given me a vision and dream to see a team of college students learning, growing, and leading in a similar way that Joel had led me when I was in college, and it seemed to be lining up perfectly with this ministry. Too certain that this job would work out, my now-husband and I decided to stay and settle in Waco.

The return from our honeymoon was met with a "no" from this ministry, and I was *devastated*. Armed with an MDiv, I found myself managing the coffee shop that I had been a barista at during my grad school years. You know what seminary didn't prepare me for? Analyzing cost of goods sold. I felt like I was drowning.

"But I thought you said . . ." I found myself praying again and again and again. Once again, I doubted if I knew my Shepherd's voice.

4. WHAT GIVES YOU JOY AND WHAT'S MOST CHALLENGING IN YOUR WORK?

Again, it would take much more space than I can give here to tell the myriads of stories of how Jesus was teaching, growing, comforting, and leading me in this season that, at the time, felt wasted. I kept serving at my church. I kept leading worship for the ministry that told me "No." The waiting was hard. The uncertainty and doubt were grueling. And then what felt like all at once, *thirteen years after I first sensed a call to ministry*, my worship pastor approached me about joining staff, and the local ministry approached me about building a student-led worship team. These two areas are the most joyful experiences that I have in this season. To work day in and day out for the church body that I love so much is the greatest honor. That student-led college worship team is my absolute pride and joy. I tear up just thinking about them. As I write this, I am only one year into full-time vocational ministry, but as I look back, I can see that every step of the way was what Paul calls a "living sacrifice." Admittedly, that "living sacrifice" often came kicking and screaming, but Jesus has continued to be my sanity and clarity every step of the way.

5. WHAT ADVICE DO YOU WISH SOMEONE HAD GIVEN YOU ABOUT YOUR CALL/MINISTRY?

I wish that I could take fifteen-year-old Jessica to coffee. I wish I could sit across from her awkward, insecure, sassy self and assure her that she heard her Shepherd right. I wish I could tell her to take heart and to be patient. I wish I could make her take piano lessons (to this day I am still such a mediocre musician). But instead, I will settle for encouraging you, dear sister, whoever you are. If you hear the quiet and lovely voice of your Shepherd calling you to serve his people in song, listen to him. To be sure, worship ministry involves lots of tangible skills like set preparation, Planning Center, the proper way to roll XLRs, and the number system. Learn those things. Grow in your craft and skill. But do not wait for an "official" ministry title to invite others to "taste and see that the Lord is good." Let the entirety of your life be a service given unto the Lord. Worship him in the way you pour out praise *and* in the way you pour your coffee.

"I am sure of this, that he who started a good work in you will carry it on to completion until the day of Christ Jesus" (Philippians 1:6, CSB).

III
Calling in Other Ministries

15
AUTHORSHIP
Michelle Reyes

Michelle Reyes is a culture and business coach and a professor of cultural engagement at Wheaton College. She is the award-winning author of *Becoming All Things: How Small Changes Lead to Lasting Connections across Cultures.*

1. HOW DID YOU GET INTERESTED IN YOUR FIELD/MINISTRY?

I've been writing stories on the edges of sticky notes and between the lines of my spiral notebooks since I could first hold a pencil. If we could go back in time to my second-grade class, you'd see me at my desk, homework complete, scribbling a new story to tell my friends at recess. Some people just know what they were born to do. I was born to write. One time, a teacher sent my report card home saying, "Michelle is a gifted student, but she writes too many stories." Even as a young kid, I felt proud that stories just seemed to bubble up inside of me, that words would ooze from me.

I've always seen the world through the lens of story, even now as a thirty-seven-year-old woman. Beginning in college, writing became a way to process the world. I'd have a spare notebook and pen (I've always loved a good ballpoint pen) to write down my thoughts, whether about my own personal life or the events raging in the world, and rearrange them until both they and the world around me started to make sense.

Perhaps it was only natural that as I entered ministry with my husband, I wanted to write about our experiences, not just to document what we were doing, but to show fellow ministers and practitioners how they too could find cross-cultural success as they served in their contexts. This is the reason I've written two books (*Becoming All Things* and *The Race-Wise Family*) plus countless articles. I'm an Enneagram 8, a doer by nature, someone that sees a problem and wants to help. Writing is my medium to help people, to critically engage with the world around me, and to encourage and equip folks to learn from my experiences.

2. HOW DID YOU PROCESS YOUR CALL?

For the longest time, I assumed that writing would just be a hobby for me, not a professional career path. I'm a bicultural Indian American. There are expectations in my cultural community for what jobs Indians should have and a writer generally isn't one of them. I'll never forget the day I told my parents that I wanted to get a degree in writing and become a writer. I was in sixth grade, and I can still remember their faces—sheet white, like they'd seen a ghost.

I don't hold anything against my parents. What I experienced as a child is so common—wanting to do something different from your parents, being misunderstood until you prove to them you can be successful. It's the plight of a trailblazer, of charting a new path for your family. But this is also the reason that I really didn't become a professional writer until I was almost thirty years old, because I didn't want to disappoint my family. I didn't want to go against the family. If you come from a cultural background where collectivism is of high value, you understand what I'm talking about here. I processed a lot of my desire to write on my own, and I thank God for giving me the personality that I have (one with a lot of grit and resilience) to pursue my dream career even when no one else understood why.

3. WHO HELPED YOU DISCERN YOUR CALL?

I'm a firm believer that God shuts doors we're not supposed to walk through. My first stint in academia came crashing down in 2018 when the liberal arts university I taught at went through extensive budget cuts. Seemingly overnight I lost my professorship. I was four months pregnant and found myself asking, "Well, now what?" God's answer came almost immediately thereafter: "Write."

When I told my husband where I felt God was leading me, he said something to the effect of, "Yes! You were born to write!" To say he's been my biggest cheerleader and supporter is an understatement.

By the following summer I was in the throes of motherhood with a newborn, writing chapters of my book on the notes app on my phone (often between one and three a.m.), and I knew this was exactly where God wanted me to be. I would have never been able to write Christian nonfiction had I stayed in academia. It was a wild transition, but looking back, the right one, and God knew what he was doing long before I caught wind of his plan. And I'm grateful for my husband and other close friends who quickly named my gift of writing and supported me throughout the process.

4. WHAT GIVES YOU JOY AND WHAT'S MOST CHALLENGING IN YOUR WORK?

I've made the argument on several occasions that everyone has one of four cultural personalities—explorer, critic, enthusiast, and connector. I'm a cultural connector. I absolutely find my groove in helping people connect across cultures, foster cultural inclusion, and really be all that they were made to be as cultural image bearers. Seeing people thrive with their unique God-given cultural leadership style and lead and serve people of other cultures in gracious, thoughtful ways lights me up. Being a cultural connector is the reason why, beyond writing, I'm also a culture and business coach. I will never shame someone for where they're at in their cultural journey. No question is too silly. And every person, regardless of ethnic heritage or skin color, has an important role to play in cultural engagement today. If you want to leverage culturally inclusive strategies to have a greater impact and reach where you live, work, and lead, I'll help you get there.

Regarding challenges: we live in an age of outrage where people aren't always the nicest when it comes to engaging cross-culturally. I look at the noise on the internet and just shake my head. Not only are we not making progress in these conversations, but our mudslinging is causing us to slide backward. We're making people more fearful and less likely to engage in culturally related topics because we've shamed them into a hole they never want to come back out of. My greatest challenge is often taking that heat myself and learning how to respond in ways that are gracious, while also helping those who have been truly hurt and wounded to find cultural healing so they can become resilient and keep going.

5. WHAT ADVICE DO YOU WISH SOMEONE HAD GIVEN YOU ABOUT YOUR CALL/MINISTRY?

There is no straight path to success. There have been times I've looked back on my life with regret. Sometimes I wish I had been an English major or writing major in college. Maybe that would have accelerated my writing career. But then I think about the path God has taken me on, the unique educational experiences I've had, and how I implement that in an interdisciplinary way with my life experiences through my writing. There's no one out there like me who writes like me, with my style and perspective. I think a lot of times college students put too much pressure on themselves to "get it right" the first time with their majors and career choices. But God can take any starting point and guide you where you want to go. Now I tell college-aged students, "Don't sweat it. Just do something. God will do the rest." I wish someone had told this to me early in my career. I probably would have had less anxiety and frustration over what I was doing with my life.

Some of the best advice someone gave me was to aim for failure. It's the kind of advice that makes you scratch your head at first. Like, what? Failure? The idea behind aiming for failure is that we won't get anywhere in life if we play small. For example, as a writer, if I only tried to write one article at a time and only submit it to one magazine for publication, my chances of getting published are slim to none. But, as a mentor encouraged me, I should write regularly and widely and submit as often as I can. I aim for one hundred rejections a year, in fact. Because if I'm getting rejected one hundred times that means I've submitted articles at least one hundred times. At the very least, my writing is going to improve from all that writing practice. But more likely is that someone, somewhere, is going to pick up my work and I'm going to get my big first break. And that's exactly what happened. The rest is history.

16
COUNSELING
Amy Gupta

Amy Gupta works as a therapist for Discover Counseling. Over the past twenty-five years, she has served in numerous areas of ministry, including missions and pastoral work.

1. HOW DID YOU GET INTERESTED IN YOUR FIELD/MINISTRY?

My call to counseling was not a clear "voice from God" experience. The first time I thought about a degree in counseling I was serving as a college minister at Menlo Church in the Bay Area. It was a great ministry with hundreds of students from Stanford University as well as some from Santa Clara and other Bay Area colleges. Within our ministry, there were many students struggling with things like eating disorders, personality disorders, depression, anxiety, and cutting behaviors. My call to more formally study counseling came as I questioned whether I was qualified to give wise counsel while ministering to these students and experienced concern that I could do real damage in giving bad advice. I remembered back to when I was young, and my mom met with our church pastor, and then she came home to enforce what seemed like the worst possible advice. To be fair, I don't remember what that pastor's advice was, so it might not have been all that bad. But for my kid-self, whatever it was, it was bad enough to make me think twice about speaking into college students' mental health struggles without more education on them. This experience stuck with me when I went to seminary and was what motivated me to get a counseling MA in the process.

2. HOW DID YOU PROCESS YOUR CALL?

My first vocational call was ministry. It was a challenge to respond to this call because I came to faith in a Southern Baptist youth group, where I felt discouraged from pursuing my call to pastoral ministry. I tried being a missionary first in the parachurch world, but God was still tugging me toward seminary. Then I tried teaching high school Spanish at a Christian school, but still felt drawn toward seminary. While teaching Spanish, I started visiting nearby seminaries on the weekends. It was tough for me to come to terms with a call that I knew the people that had mentored me in the faith would not support. I remember thinking, "God, you could call me to be the president of the United States and it would be easier than this."

As I looked at seminaries, I met someone doing college ministry through Menlo Church. It was a parachurch-style ministry operating in a church—a model that sounded interesting to me and a great way to postpone my seminary heart tug a little longer. But God knew what he was doing. At Menlo I saw women pastors for the first time. They were women like me, not power-hungry feminists aggressively on a mission to dismantle the patriarchy as someone had gotten into my head, but just women, serving as leaders of the church—on a mission, yes, but focused on serving God. The replacement of the patriarchy with a better framework is God's job. It was in this space that I finally began to embrace my own call to ministry. I was finally willing to attend seminary, and I chose to attend Gordon-Conwell Theological Seminary for a master of divinity and a master of arts in counseling.

Right before my very first seminary class began at Gordon-Conwell, there was a preaching conference. Up on the stage was this handsome second-year student leading worship. He had a beautiful voice, the best smile, and he was strumming a guitar in cargo shorts and a polo. Long story short, we got married. Both of us were individually wrestling through what role women should play in the church and through deep study of Scripture we found God's approval of women serving in all church capacities. As we finished our degrees, we had our first baby girl, Simryn.

We left Massachusetts for England two months later and began a ten-year adventure around the world pursuing my husband, Nijay's, call to teach, beginning with his PhD at Durham University in England. During the next eight years of moving from place to place, I worked in various church jobs and other professions. In England I was the residence director of our international graduate housing. We had our son, Aidan, while still living in England. After Nijay finished his PhD, we moved our family of four to Ohio for Nijay to adjunct at Ashland Seminary. We were there for a year when Nijay was hired at Seattle Pacific University. In Seattle our youngest daughter, Libby, was born. While there I served as a pastor to young adults at First Free Methodist Church. After two years at SPU, we moved to Philadelphia, where Nijay worked at Eastern University. Four days after arriving in Philadelphia, our fifteen-month-old baby girl, Libby, was diagnosed with leukemia. The counseling job I had lined up was back-burnered as we cared for her through the next three years of chemotherapy. (Sidenote: Libby is now thirteen and thriving. Thank you, Jesus!)

Though I went to seminary primarily for my MDiv and saw my counseling degree as supplemental, I thoroughly enjoyed diving into psychology and learning how to help families thrive. I loved the study of human development so much that while we were living in England, I continued my studies in counseling and earned an additional two certificates in early childhood development. Being inspired by how significant early childhood is for our faith and lives, I tried my hand at being a children's pastor when we made our final move to Portland. In my six months serving as a children's pastor, I gained a tremendous amount of respect for church leaders working in that age group. Children's ministry requires individuals with so much talent—recruiting, managing, and encouraging volunteers, preparing messages, producing entertaining skits, organizing crafts, navigating how to care for kids with special needs, organizing summer VBS-like programs, directing kids' choir (aka "worship with hand motions"), welcoming new families, etc. Unfortunately, I found my position on staff very discouraging. I was only brought into conversation when there was a question about childcare. If the church had been well led, I probably would have stayed on the team for the mission, regardless of my discouragement. But the church has since gone under, and its building sold to become a Hindu temple.

After many jobs—among them a teacher, a missionary, a residence director, a track coach, and a pastor—I finally attempted to open my own private practice for marriage therapy. While living in Seattle I had begun studying the Gottman Method of marriage therapy, and Nijay and I over the next few years began applying the Gottman Method to our marriage. We loved how it improved our life together. Eight moves in ten years with three children born and one diagnosed with cancer is a lot for any marriage, so we needed more support. After watching the Gottman Method help us feel like we were winning at marriage again, I felt inspired to help others win through my own private practice utilizing the Gottman Method. For anyone searching for a great marriage book, I highly recommend *The Seven Principles for Making Marriage Work* by John Gottman and Nan Silver. Though I was enjoying therapy, I decided to take on another part-time ministry job as a youth pastor because we wanted our kids in a neighborhood youth group. My plan was to run my counseling business part-time and youth pastor part-time. But when the COVID outbreak happened it was too difficult to maintain both jobs, so I focused on youth ministry. Libby's cancer had prepared me well to navigate the COVID rules, so I was able to make a quick pivot to all the Portland requirements for COVID days. I got to see God grow the youth group through the COVID season. And after getting the youth group through the COVID season, I stepped away from the role. I then supported a different youth group as interim youth pastor for a season. But I ultimately decided to return my focus to counseling so my own three kids could stay put in one church for their remaining school years.

3. WHO HELPED YOU DISCERN YOUR CALL?

My different jobs through various moves felt random and disorganized to me until I joined a women's cohort and worked out my mission statement. Coming up with a mission statement helped me reconcile all my experiences as anything but random. After a beautiful year of self-discovery, I connected the dots of my journey. Through the support of my WIML (Women in Ministry Leadership) cohort, I was able to find clarity for my call. My calling was to help people find holistic well-being. And to the point of this essay, sorting out my mission statement helped me understand how counseling fit that call. Counseling helps people grow into Christ followers in all facets of their lives. I highly recommend coming up with a mission statement for your life if you have not yet done so. Thinking deeply through a mission statement was such a productive self-reflection to help me know myself better as well as my vocational direction. Knowing my mission statement has freed me up to say more yeses and nos without as much stress about the shoulds and shouldn'ts. It has helped me to better understand what I value in the work I choose.

4. WHAT GIVES YOU JOY AND WHAT'S MOST CHALLENGING IN YOUR WORK?

As much as counseling is a step away from church ministry for me, it has truly been more of a continuation of it. I delight in helping people know and share God's love better. Knowing God's love better happens from a good sermon; so too it happens in a counseling office. I have been able to spend way more one-on-one time with people as a counselor than time allowed as a pastor. I have been able to see behind the curtain of people's lives and help them get unstuck from stuck places. I get to help people better love their spouses, their parents, their friends and workmates, themselves, and their God. I get to help people calm their anxious hearts and find peace in their spirit and with others. I feel like an interior designer, helping people shine light in dark places and renovate their hearts and lives with the fresh decor of God's choosing.

It's been an absolute delight to see how many of the most effective theories of counseling agree with biblical teachings. Whether it's acceptance theory, cognitive behavioral therapy, or emotion-focused therapy, biblical principles are proven to work well again and again. I watch how God's instructions play out in the lives of those I serve through therapy, and let me tell you, God's rules really are for our good, and not just his glory. As much as I struggled to want to obey him when I was younger, looking back at my life, I see that God has blessed me in keeping his commandments and has spared me from so much harm too. And I see the same things playing out in others' lives. I like to call the Ten Commandments "best practices" because reframing them from rules to wise instruction makes it easier for my rebellious heart to follow them.

Counseling has been such a perfect profession with boundaries while raising a family. I remember hearing someone say that you can have it all as a mom, but not all at once. This has been true in my life. Things have come in seasons. Though I feel like I took a longer time out from really pursuing my career than I wanted, my kids are now older, and the juggling act of parenting has gotten more manageable for working. I love wearing the different hats of life. And counseling has helped me wear them all better, with deeper gratitude and reflection for each role I play.

This last year I transitioned from a private practice to a counseling group. I was nervous I wasn't running my own business well. In retrospect, I was doing fine. But I have still appreciated the change because having Christian workmates and not managing as much administration myself is a nice benefit of being in a group. (Administration would have been listed under my counseling challenges otherwise.) It's fun to be on a team of people committed to bringing hope and healing to those they serve. As part of a group practice, I am able to quickly triage challenging cases with other therapists for more insight into how to support clients. Plus, I have great workmates to encourage me when I process my emotions.

5. WHAT ADVICE DO YOU WISH SOMEONE HAD GIVEN YOU ABOUT YOUR CALL/MINISTRY?

Though I love the clear time limits and boundaries created by the framework of therapy, they can also be a challenge. There are physical and emotional challenges to hourly appointments. It can be exhausting to have only five-minute breaks between sessions in a day filled with people's traumas. Plus, sitting hour after hour can become monotonous. I try to exercise before and after work to ameliorate the tiredness that comes from sitting all day. At times it can be emotionally tricky to not take clients' problems home with me. And if I don't get enough sleep, I don't always have the energy to show up well emotionally for my friends and family after a day of work.

My road into counseling was not a straight one but has been filled with twists and turns and pit stops along the way. As much as a clear-cut career path would have been simpler, I appreciated the adventure of this journey too. And hopefully all the stops along the way have made me a more informed therapist, better able to serve my clients. What I know is true is that regardless of my experiences, God will take all of it and use it for his glory and my good.

17
CULTURAL ENGAGEMENT
Katie Frugé

Katie Frugé is the director of the Center for Cultural Engagement and of the Christian Life Commission for the Baptist General Convention of Texas. In her role, she helps Texas Baptists think biblically about cultural, moral, and political issues.

1. HOW DID YOU GET INTERESTED IN YOUR FIELD/MINISTRY?

When I think about a younger me sitting in the church pew with my feet dangling, I mostly recall sermons about what Christians need to believe. However, in the preacher's illustrations, I remember most involved stories about good trees producing good fruit: Christians loving their neighbors as themselves.

It was not until my late teens that I learned there's a word for this that pairs with orthodoxy. The theological term is orthopraxy. I immediately felt drawn to opportunities to discuss orthopraxy and try to be more authentically Christlike.

Good theology is critical and should be carefully crafted and considered under submission to the Holy Spirit and in accordance with Scripture, but faith without works is dead. Some might read cultural engagement and think of cultural wars and ideological battlefields, but for me, it has been an opportunity to live out the gospel message. Christian engagement leads to reconciliation and healing in relationships, communities, and policies.

Cultural engagement means stepping away from the online wars of the day and going into the places where Jesus instructed us to go. I have never been one to engage in keyboard warrior battles, but from an early age, I felt compelled to physically go to places where I knew I could make a difference. In high school, I committed the book of James to memory and was deeply moved to see the importance of right living as the expression of faith.

From advocating in the halls of the Capitol to serving a hungry child in a food desert, I have found cultural engagement to be a way to live out the words of James 2:18 (NIV): "You have faith; I have deeds. Show me your faith without deeds, and I will show you my faith by my deeds."

2. HOW DID YOU PROCESS YOUR CALL?

I began sensing a call to ministry when I was sixteen years old. Up to this point I had been born into Baptist church life. Neither of my parents was in ministry, but we made it to church three times a week. By sixteen I was happy to be singing on the youth group worship team.

One thing that remained constant from birth to participating in my youth group is the women I saw in leadership or was taught about. These leaders were mainly pastor's wives or missionaries. As I began to process feeling called to ministry, I only recall three options: pastor's wife, missionary, or both. At sixteen, I remember being open to all three while knowing the only one I could control was going into the mission field.

As I approached college, I felt aimless and unclear about where and how God might have me serve. Unclear of my future, I was an undeclared major for the first two years at university. Since I attended a Baptist university, part of the core requirements included introductory courses on the Old and New Testament. My first real exposure to theological training sparked a fire in my heart to know more. I declared a major in Christian Studies, sensing God's direction to continue my education in theology.

My experience is that God's calling in my life continues to develop and move as seasons of life change. I am only semi-joking when I explain my life as a series of stumbling through the open doors God calls me through—trusting in the Lord to guide me every step of the journey, whether I know where I'm headed or not.

3. WHO HELPED YOU DISCERN YOUR CALL?

I have had the privilege of growing up with an incredibly supportive family my entire life. At sixteen, I shared with my parents and grandparents that I sensed God's calling upon my life. Immediately, they shared their own observations of how they had sensed God's hand in my life, unique among my peers and siblings.

When I transitioned to college, I felt aimless and unclear about where my calling might direct me. My family affirmed God's hand in my life and never wavered in their patience and support as I struggled to understand where God was calling me. I met my husband in an Introduction to Greek class in college. As our relationship developed and grew deeper, his support of my call to ministry also grew. By my senior year of college, we were engaged, and he agreed to move to Texas to support my top choice for seminary education.

In the decades since I have continued to be indebted to the support structure God has placed in my life. They have patiently, lovingly, and kindly walked with me as I discerned how God was calling me to be a part of growing his kingdom on earth.

Professors throughout my theological training were also profoundly important. I was a sophomore in college when someone called me a "budding theologian," the first time I had ever heard that phrase used to describe me. Others speaking out loud about what they see in you is impactful and can be empowering. It does not necessarily mean speaking words of affirmation. Once a professor shared with me his disappointment with my work—not because it was bad or poorly done, but because he believed I could do better. He was right, and I did better. He saw something in me that I could not see at the time. I'm the product of many men and women who saw something in me, supported me, and invested in my calling.

4. WHAT GIVES YOU JOY AND WHAT'S MOST CHALLENGING IN YOUR WORK?

The fruit of true cultural engagement is cultural transformation. It is my joy and privilege to stand in the tradition of cultural transformers who led the abolitionist movement, opened hospitals and orphanages, started food ministries, and countless other ways we have seen Christians serving as the hands and feet of Jesus.

My greatest joy comes when I see the truth of Jesus's proclamation that the kingdom of heaven has already come. It is tempting to look at the world and be discouraged. Wars and rumors of war, political polarization, and extremism on the left and right are all constant in the daily news cycle. Still, even in challenging times, I find incredible joy in seeing pockets of the kingdom grow. It's the joy of helping support legislation that upholds and validates the dignity of individuals with intellectual disabilities. It's the joy of seeing a once-run-down part of a town transformed into a thriving community because God gave someone a vision for what could be. The joy of watching the kingdom of God grow is the stream God places in the wasteland.

The greatest challenge is the increasing polarization of ideas today. The zeitgeist of our day places issues in ideological buckets. It feels like the American mind is losing its ability to recognize nuance and sensitivity on the most basic issues. To disagree is to be hostile; nothing short of full affirmation is acceptable.

Cultural engagement quickly drifts into culture war with a militant spirit to crush the opposition, standing in stark contrast to the Lamb who was slain before the foundation of the world. More than ever, we need God's children to engage in the work of reconciliation and restoration of true shalom.

5. WHAT ADVICE DO YOU WISH SOMEONE HAD GIVEN YOU ABOUT YOUR CALL/MINISTRY?

First, I wish someone had told me to spend more time preparing for the logistical and administrative reality of Christian leadership. Seminary is a wonderful time for receiving theological training, but often we skimp on the basics of leadership and how to operate a ministry. The result is (1) on-the-job training or (2) leaders who are incredible at doing ministry but awful at leading. Neither is ideal. There are plenty of good resources available on leadership training and administrative budgets. I wish someone had told me how vital those skills would be in addition to the importance of my theological training. A good leader should have a comprehensive understanding of all the jobs and work done by the ministry they oversee. It does not mean you can do it as well as they do or that you know the minutiae of the assignment, but it should be accurate and complete. If a leader only has a half-understanding of what a ministry does operationally, they make choices with far-reaching unintended consequences. A leader with administrative and financial literacy skills helps cultivate more effective ministry outcomes for everyone. Effective leadership can be a way of living out your call to ministry.

Second, learn early to differentiate when you need to push hard and work diligently unto the Lord and when it is time to take a break. Ministry is one of the most nonstop of all vocational callings. It's not your usual nine-to-five. It can be physically, emotionally, and spiritually exhausting. A critical piece to a life in ministry is knowing when to say "no" to wonderful ministry opportunities. Those called to ministry are also called to rest. The Sabbath was made for us. We follow God's own example when we set aside time to rest. It should be a regular part of our lifestyle. This is one of my greatest weaknesses, and I have had to learn through painful experiences the price the body and soul pay when we neglect to rest. Overextending in ministry work will also result in less fruitful results. When ministry is coming from fumes, the aroma of exhaustion is evident. Faithfully stewarding God's calling includes making margin for rest and knowing when to say "no" in ministry.

18

HOMEMAKING

Sarah S. Kim

Sarah S. Kim is a former InterVarsity staff worker at Boston University. She pioneered the Asian American Christian Fellowship at Boston College.

1. HOW DID YOU GET INTERESTED IN YOUR FIELD/MINISTRY?

From a young age, all I wanted was to change the world. I would see World Vision commercials on TV of starving children, and it would break my heart. I made my parents sponsor a child and wrote personal letters to a boy named Jesús for many years until my parents eventually stopped sending money. As young as I was, I really believed I could make this world a better place.

I believe I have made the world better but not in the way I had originally conceived. I've changed a small piece of the world by being a homemaker and stay-at-home mom. It may seem strange to think of being a wife, mother, daughter, sister, or friend as a ministry, but it is. If you asked my younger self about this, I would probably have said no. I would have said those things are parts of your identity, but they are not a ministry.

My husband and I got married in 2002, so at the time of this writing, we have been married twenty-three years. I have a good friend who told me recently that all she ever wanted to be in life was a mom. I always knew I wanted to have children one day. By God's grace, I have enjoyed being a mother to our three sons for over seventeen years. Besides the first three years of our marriage, I have never had a paid job. The last two decades have been spent as a wife, mother, daughter, sister, friend, Sunday school teacher, and baseball coach, among other random things.

2. HOW DID YOU PROCESS YOUR CALL?

After graduating from Boston University, I came on staff with InterVarsity and pioneered a chapter at Boston College. At the time, I believed I was going to be doing this work for the rest of my life.

It was during this time that I learned how to study the Bible, and the greatest commandments in Matthew 22 "to love God and love our neighbors" became central and foremost in my faith. I loved student ministry and couldn't imagine doing anything else. I had a clear vision of helping college students learn to study the word of God and how they could use their studies and careers to impact our world for God's kingdom.

I began dating my husband toward the end of my second year of serving with InterVarsity. He was entering his last year of seminary and making plans for post-graduation. When he told me that he wanted us to get married and pursue a PhD in Edinburgh, Scotland, my first reaction was, "Um, no." I was certain that God wanted me to serve with IV, so he could go by himself, get his degree, and if we were both still single after he finished, we could consider getting married. Well, he responded, "Won't you at least take some time to pray about it?" I couldn't say no, so I prayed. For the third time in my life, I heard God speak to me, "I see you, Sarah. I will take care of you. Marry him and go."

Being the independent young woman that I was, I didn't want to give up my career and follow my husband. Everything inside of me rebelled against this, but God's words for me were so precise in addressing my greatest fears, I knew that it was the right decision and what God wanted for me.

3. WHO HELPED YOU DISCERN YOUR CALL?

The simple answer is God did.

As soon as we moved to Scotland, our newly minted marriage was put to the test. I was living in a different country where I didn't understand how anything worked. I had left a job I loved, left my friends and family, and had literally nothing to do. When we arrived, Matt jumped right into his studies. I couldn't work until I got a work visa, which would take some time. So I went from being busy all the time in college to doing nothing.

To fill the time, I read on average between three and four books per week. I cooked and baked and baked again. We lived in a small apartment building with mostly elderly people, so I divided up what I had baked and left packages of baked goods in front of their doors. Once I got my work visa, I signed up with a temporary job agency and took any work I could get. My first job was at the Body Shop on Princes Street in downtown Edinburgh where I had to learn how to put makeup on women even though I had never worn makeup in my life. I worked various retail jobs after that. I also helped old people with their grocery shopping and counted cars coming in and out of parking lots (as paid work). Little did I know then that God was laying foundational pieces for the rest of my life.

The thought that ran through my head during this three-year period was, "What am I doing? Are you sure this is what you wanted, God? Had I stayed in Boston and not gotten married, I could have been doing so much more with my life." However, what God taught me during this time was probably the most profound lesson I could have ever learned.

I don't think God places value in things the way humans do. I felt like I was doing insignificant tasks, but God very specifically showed me that there is nothing insignificant to ministry. More specifically, *there is no one who is insignificant.* All those places I worked, all those people I interacted with, God was calling me to be his vessel. He was calling me to be faithful no matter what I was doing. He was calling me to work hard, to give my best, to be a light in the darkness wherever I was, in whatever I was doing.

What I was doing didn't matter as much as the attitude in which I was doing it. This was the greatest lesson I could have learned before having children. Why? Feeling insignificant as a stay-at-home mom can often be a great struggle.

4. WHAT GIVES YOU JOY AND WHAT'S MOST CHALLENGING IN YOUR WORK?

I think the hardest of the battles that we face today, whether you are a man or woman, is the battle that goes on in our minds. The grass being greener on the other side is probably the greatest psychological weapon used against humans—along with fear. Being content exactly where we are is a lifelong struggle that most people don't come to terms with unless they are a terminally ill patient faced with the imminent reality of death. Living life out of a place of fear is exactly where the enemy wants us. There is a great sense of awe and wonder that happens when you become a parent, but there can also be this great sense of fear.

As I stated earlier, when you are a stay-at-home mom, the enemy attacks with feeling insignificant. We feel like an unproductive member of society, sitting on the bench while the rest of the world is contributing and winning. We scroll in between changing diapers, doing laundry, cooking, and cleaning, and see others "truly living." I know many working moms face their own challenges and battles: feeling judged for choosing work over family, missing out on different school events because of work, dealing with the stress of balancing work and home life.

Although I struggled at times with being "just a mom," my greatest challenges relate to fear. All three of my children had several health challenges growing up. All three had febrile seizures. They had varying degrees of food allergies, asthma, and eczema. It just felt like they were sick all the time. I never slept soundly out of fear that one of my boys would have a seizure while they were sleeping. This laid the foundation for other fears to creep in. Since my boys had so many health issues, I felt like I had to be prepared for any and every crisis, including war, famine, poverty, etc. In our family we called it preparing for the "Zombie Apocalypse."

I could never feel fully prepared so there was always a part of me that lived in a place of fear.

Three years ago, when we moved to Texas, in God's mercy, I faced the greatest challenge I had ever encountered, and I was totally and completely unprepared for it. It began innocently with my husband not sleeping well from all the stress that came with moving across the country. But then it took a turn that I could not have imagined. The trouble sleeping turned into complete insomnia, which turned worse. In short, our primary care physician prescribed something for sleep that made my husband suicidal. That turned into six months of completely uncharted territory for me and my boys. At the lowest point, I believed that my husband was either going to kill himself or would have to be hospitalized for the rest of his life.

It was a week or so into this battle that lasted six months that I was on the phone with my pastor from the church we had been attending in Massachusetts. In that moment, I knew that I was in a dark pit like the ones that King David always asked God to rescue him from. I had this terrible feeling that the pit was going to get much deeper. My pastor said, "Daughter of God most high, God wants you to cast out all fear. You will not be able to face what is coming if you are living in fear." When he said this, I knew it was God speaking to me through him.

So I prayed and claimed freedom from all the fears that were binding me. Now, did I completely stop fearing after that moment? Of course not, but there was a marked difference in me. And whenever those familiar feelings came along, I was and am now able to cast them at the feet of Jesus. I remember the first time my boys experienced "No Fear" mom. They asked if they could ride their bikes to the park on their own and explore our new neighborhood. Normally, I would only let them go if I was with them, even though they were old enough to ride on their own (high school and middle school). When I said yes, they didn't know what to say at first. Then they kept asking, "By ourselves? Are you sure?"

One thing I have been thankful for is that I have always been able to talk to my children, something I didn't get to experience much of growing up in an Asian family. I love that I got to share with my boys how I had been enslaved to fear for so long, but that God had set me free. This is probably the best part of being a stay-at-home mom. I get to talk with them about every aspect of life.

It was a very conscious decision on my part to raise my boys this way. When I was younger, my mother always tried to hide things from me because she didn't want me to experience any unnecessary hardship. So we never talked about hard things. I did not want my boys to grow up that way. I wanted them to learn early on and gain wisdom from the mistakes I had made and from others' mistakes. I didn't want to hide the hard things in life, because life is hard for everyone. By talking to them I wanted them to recognize and see God's faithfulness in every circumstance. At the ages of seventeen, sixteen, and thirteen, they still have a lot of life to live and a lot to learn. But I'm extremely grateful for the foundation that has been set for them.

The worst or most challenging part of being a parent is that we can't control anything. We wonder, Will they have friends? Will they make the right choices? Will they follow Jesus? There are endless questions and things we can worry about. It is so hard to lay all of that at the feet of Jesus, to not fear and to simply trust. All we can do as parents is lay the best foundation we can for our children and then pray constantly. Never underestimate your prayers for your children. From the time my oldest was in my belly and for all three kids, I have prayed the same prayer: for God to grant them wisdom, to make good choices, and to bring good people into their lives.

As I sit here writing this chapter, I am at the gym watching my three boys play basketball with five of their friends. Afterward, I'll take them to go get something to eat and then one friend will spend the night with us. The friend has requested that I make my "friend famous" fried chicken sandwiches.

This is what I love to do. I love that I get to be a part of their lives and their friends' lives. I get to cheer for them from the sidelines, pray for them, talk with them about our world, politics, friendship, or relationships. I count it a blessing that I can attend every game.

I confess that I still have moments when I see the piles of dirty laundry and dishes in the sink and think, "Is this it, Lord?" Then I remember what God taught me years ago: it is about being faithful wherever God places us at any moment in time.

There's a song by Christian artist Josiah Queen called "Garden in Manhattan." I love these lyrics:

A garden in Manhattan
A flower in the concrete
If that's where you want me.

5. WHAT ADVICE DO YOU WISH SOMEONE HAD GIVEN YOU ABOUT YOUR CALL/MINISTRY?

Pain and suffering are part of our Christian journey. This is an act of God's grace and mercy. It is true that we learn more from our hardships than from seasons of calm. If you look at the example of Jesus and his disciples, if you are living the Christian life in the way it was intended, it will be the hardest road you will ever journey on. The world will tell us, Do what's right for you; You don't deserve this; Who cares about other people?

When we were going through that battle with my husband, all those negative thoughts bombarded me every day. On a day when I didn't think I could take any more, God showed me a brief picture in my mind of how much Jesus suffered on this earth—how Jesus suffered and endured even though he didn't deserve any of it. I realized in that moment that our calling is the same. It is a calling to endure and not give up.

There was a verse that God gave me shortly after that struggle and it's stuck with me since: "Finally, brothers [and sisters], whatever is true, whatever is honorable, whatever is just, whatever is pure, whatever is lovely, whatever is commendable, if there is any excellence, if there is anything worthy of praise, think about these things. What you have learned and received and heard and seen in me—practice these things, and the God of peace will be with you" (Philippians 4:8–9, ESV).

I hope, fellow sister, that no matter what is going on in the world around us you would think of these things and have the peace of God. Faithfulness is doing what God has called you to do, even in the seemingly insignificant things, for his glory. In the end, everything we do is for him alone.

19
HUMAN TRAFFICKING
INTERVENTION
Bonnie J. Gatchell

Bonnie J. Gatchell cofounded Route One Ministry in 2010, a nonprofit serving sexually exploited and trafficked women and young girls (www.lovedbyrouteone .org). In 2016, she was invited to the TEDx stage and ordained by the EPC.

1. HOW DID YOU GET INTERESTED IN YOUR FIELD/MINISTRY?

Some would argue that I came out of the womb fighting for justice and women's rights. My specific calling and use of that passion came when I met my first stripper, Sally. Sally was sixty-two years old and still working in the strip club. She looked sixty-two, with C-section scars, crow's feet, and tired arms and legs. I was awakened to the reality of trafficking and exploitation here in the United States.

In 2010, I graduated from Gordon-Conwell Theological Seminary with an MDiv. After searching for the traditional pastorate, I decided to take part-time employment, return to Gordon-Conwell for a ThM in church history, and spend the next year exploring where God may be leading. A few months into this search, a past boss asked me to sit on the board of directors for an anti-trafficking nonprofit he was launching—Priceless International. At the time, this sounded boring to me. The anti-trafficking work felt distant, and effecting such work as a board member felt even more distant.

Nonetheless, I was intrigued by the possibility of serving vulnerable women, so I asked a friend who served as a board member to meet. My classmate, Laurelann Copp, joined us for this conversation. Laurelann asked, "I work at a Christian high school. How can high school students address the issue of trafficking here, on the North Shore?" Sarah replied, "Make baskets and bring them to strippers working in strip clubs on Christmas Eve."

My heart leaped. The next day, I googled strip clubs near the church I attended. I found two strip clubs within two miles of the church. I called and asked the manager if we could bring baskets to the women who worked in the club on Christmas Eve. He said it sounded odd but harmless. He told me that twenty-five women were scheduled to work on Christmas Eve. I made a list of fun, gift-like items for the baskets: lip gloss, journals, coffee mugs, and other items that I would enjoy receiving.

Laurelann and other women from the church led the delivery. The women who worked at the strip club greeted them with tears in their eyes. Several wanted hugs, and one woman stated that this basket would be the only gift she received that year. We knew at that moment that there was something more nefarious and complicated than what we had understood about strip clubs or the women who worked in the clubs.

Over the following weeks, I researched how we, as a church, could connect with women on a regular basis. I found a group in Kentucky that delivered hot homemade meals to the women working in the strip clubs. The idea of connecting to women this way appealed to me, and I arranged to meet and shadow that organization. I drove to Kentucky from my parents' home in Michigan.

Once I was in Kentucky, the executive director talked me through their day-to-day, gave me a handbook, and allowed me to join her team for their Thursday outreach night. It was New Year's Eve of 2010. I had planned to be in Montreal for a thirtieth birthday party and wedding, but God had very different plans. Instead of these celebrations, I was standing in a dirty dressing room of one of twenty strip clubs located in this Kentucky town. It was here that I met Sally. Sally ran away from home at eighteen. She planned on working in the strip clubs for one summer, making money, and leaving the clubs and her family to secure a new way of life. She never left the clubs.

In this dressing room, engaging with Sally, my heart ached and leaped all at the same time. I knew God was calling me and other Christian women to enter strip clubs and build relationships with the women who work in the clubs. In the following months, Laurelann and I worked with our church to create a vision statement and safety plans, recruit volunteers, and launch Route One Ministry. We started with one strip club and four volunteers. We are now in the four largest cities in New England, serving nearly seventy women weekly. Our outreach teams have helped the women secure new employment, regain custody of their children, publish their stories, exit emergencies, find healthy churches, and more. We at Route One believe that each woman is made in the image of God. We are joyful at the opportunity to partner with churches and serve Jesus by serving women in strip clubs.

While attending seminary, I had no intention of running a women's ministry, and I am grateful for this surprise. Fifteen years later, God continues to reveal his love for the women in clubs and for me through this work and the doors he has opened. Thanks be to God!

2. HOW DID YOU PROCESS YOUR CALL?

As mentioned earlier, my call to work with sexually exploited and trafficked women came through a series of events that culminated in the dressing room of a strip club. Leaving that strip club, I knew if the church wanted to reach sexually exploited women, we would need to enter strip clubs without hurry or judgment.

I first processed this calling with Laurelann, my cofounder and fellow graduate of Gordon-Conwell. I further sought godly counsel from the elders of my church, asking for their confirmation for this calling on my life, and I connected with other women in other states who already lead strip club ministries that served sexually exploited women. Looking back, the Holy Spirit clearly led me through each step of this journey. It was Laurelann's wisdom to involve the elders of our church.

Additionally, I spent much time processing this call with the Lord privately through prayer, fasting, long walks, journaling, and conversations with godly friends. While this journey was not easy, there was never resistance in my spirit. I moved through these first few months like being carried on a spiritual conveyor belt. In 2016, I was ordained in the EPC with an out-of-bounds call to Route One and our work.

3. WHO HELPED YOU DISCERN YOUR CALL?

Discerning one's call, I believe, happens throughout one's life—or at least that is how it happened for me. Of course, there are specific details in the months and even the years leading to the birth of this work and, thus, my calling. The truth, however, is that the calling of the Holy Spirit on my life started when I was six. As a six-year-old, I would pretend that my stuffed animals and mom were my congregation, a memory silenced shortly following middle school. I highly respected our family pastor (Pastor Tim Nyhuis) and thought what he did was essential; even as a child, I understood the pastorate as someone who helped others understand and apply scripture, which spoke deeply to my core.

For college, I attended Cornerstone University in Grand Rapids, MI. Drs. Bonzo, Bustrum, and Morman all played an essential role in helping me deconstruct and reconstruct my theology around women, the church, and leadership. I entered college believing that I needed to find another way for God to use my desire for the church, study of scripture, and passion for justice; with the guidance and encouragement of each of these professors, I left feeling confident about my call.

Following college, I worked in the Dominican Republic, where I would preach my first sermon in a one-room church. Immediately after the sermon, I knew I was called to preach and to the pastorate. The following year, I started my degree at Gordon-Conwell. My time at Gordon-Conwell would lead me to North Point EPC and the birthing of Route One Ministry, a ministry uniquely crafted to reach sexually exploited women. The pastor of North Point, my roommate from GCTS, Mary Coon, and elders from Orchard EPC—Ken Glassier, Lisa and Terry Smith, and Elizabeth Cole—would all be essential to discerning my call.

4. WHAT GIVES YOU JOY, AND WHAT'S MOST CHALLENGING IN YOUR WORK?

In wanting to end on a happy note, I will start with challenges. I will share three broad and ongoing challenges:

For far too long, we have understood trafficking as something that happens "over there" and to "them." Movies like *Taken* promote such ideas. Movies like *Pretty Woman* promote a type of safety and freedom for women in prostitution that does not exist. Both promote a rescue motive. The power of shame, fear, poverty, and racism are substantial factors that hold women and young girls captive far more than ropes or cages; this includes the entrapment of strip clubs. Therefore, a challenge that has limited our opportunity to resources and even volunteers has been to help churches understand the women who work in strip clubs differently.

A second challenge is limited resources and personnel. In addition to a misunderstanding of women who work in strip clubs, there is a misunderstanding of success. It takes years to gain trust from women who have suffered so much trauma and abuse. And often this is not appealing to people. Most people want to see instant results and to volunteer for organizations that experience instant results. Our work is transitional, not transactional, which can feel counter to our industrial mindsets.

Lastly, Henri Nouwen (and later Dan Allender) rightly identified that most of us serve from our wounds, which can be good, healthy, and destructive. I grew up in a very rural impoverished area of Michigan. My childhood was filled with tumultuous events; Route One was launched to address these wounds (unknowingly). Doing good can sometimes be conflated with the wounds we have experienced as children. My challenge, which I assume is a challenge for most leaders, has been to identify those wounds. In the earlier days of the ministry, the unaddressed, unknown wounds would affect how I engaged my staff and push me to work eighty-hour work weeks. In the end, what I thought was "getting things done" was slowing tremendously the work of reaching sexually exploited women. It is essential to know these things about oneself. As leaders, once we address our wounds, we can engage the world, our work, and those who serve with us in far healthier capacities.

Now, on to my joys! My joy is this work overall. The delight that God, in his wisdom, took my feminist mind, desire for justice, and love for scripture and bundled all these into a unique calling is a profound joy.

I find joy when a dancer exits the sex industry. I find equal pleasure when volunteers understand their worth for the first time and call to the kingdom. I find joy in watching my dedicated, loyal staff put their minds and hearts on the line for the least of these and for them to lead and train others to do the same. I find joy when a buyer of sex confesses their sins and repents. I find great joy in long mornings when I make an extra-good cup of coffee and call a friend I haven't heard from in a while. And, of course, watching my nephew, Alex, grow.

5. WHAT ADVICE DO YOU WISH SOMEONE HAD GIVEN YOU ABOUT YOUR CALL/MINISTRY?

As the first child of a working-class family, I do not know if I would have heard this advice, but if I can speak it back to other firstborns and people who overcompensate by working too much, this is what I wish someone would have told me: You deserve to get paid for what you do. I worked another full-time job for the first two years and did Route One after hours when everyone had gone home. I did this partly out of a desire to do this work and partly out of a belief that getting paid for "kingdom" work was a sin. Trust your gut, even when it directs you differently than the elders in your life. Do not do it alone; find a group of at least three to four trustworthy people who will advise you, pray for you, and even wrestle with you.

20
LAW AND NONPROFIT MINISTRY

Grateful Itiowe

Grateful Itiowe is founder of Great Innovators Foundation for Transformation (GIFT), which empowers individuals and communities through visionary leadership. She inspires others as an attorney and as a faculty member at the University of Nigeria.

1. HOW DID YOU GET INTERESTED IN YOUR FIELD/MINISTRY?

Have you ever cried so hard that your body shook? I had just gotten off a long call, and the summary of the conversation was that I would no longer get the financial support I had hoped for to attend seminary in the United States. I couldn't believe it—everything had been settled. I was admitted, I had my US visa, and I had even bought my winter boots—so why would they suddenly back out? I cried so hard and loud that my neighbor's dog began barking at the strange sound. What could have caused the sudden change of mind? I soon figured it out. I was a single lady nearing thirty, a lawyer, and an MBA holder. What was I doing pursuing another master's degree now from a seminary? I faced questions like, "Do you want to become a pastor?" "Why another degree?" "Don't you want to get married?" All of these statements were rooted in societal expectations despite having seemingly good intentions.

I knew that pursuing a master's in global leadership could enhance my nonprofit ministry, but perhaps it wasn't the right time yet. With faith in God's plan, I continued lecturing at the University of Nigeria, serving at The Old Path Revival Church, and managing our family school, Good Hope Stars Schools. During this time, God comforted me with an unexpected consulting opportunity for the state government despite my young age. When God calls us to follow him, and we say, "Yes, Lord," challenges are part of the journey. Jesus's disciples, like us, experienced miracles, healing, and provision, but also faced storms, hunger, disagreements, trials, and even death.

If you assumed that following Jesus is like a perfect father-daughter road trip with nothing going wrong, think again. I've learned that following the Lord is about obedience and patience; that is, doing what he asks when and how he asks. It is also about believing that you are worthy, capable, and deserving of the opportunities he brings your way with the help of his Spirit while ignoring the lies of the devil that cause feelings of insecurity and perceived fraudulence (impostor syndrome). These lies plague many women who strive to rise above the status quo. Following involves trusting the Shepherd, knowing he understands the future, the dangers, and the best path for us that will lead us to green pastures and restore our souls.

Growing up as a pastor's kid, I witnessed my parents' dedication to helping the underprivileged and advocating for widows, orphans, and others close to God's heart. This upbringing instilled a passion to serve in that ministry and has led to the founding of my nonprofit based in Nigeria, Great Innovators Foundation for Transformation (GIFT). One significant moment involved celebrating my twentieth birthday, to the surprise of my friends, at an orphanage near my university, where I sang, gave gifts, and enjoyed time with the children. That experience made me realize my passion for bringing joy to others and glorifying God. My journey taught me to discern choices based on what brings joy to

God and me but remember, when we align our actions with God's will, the joy of obedience follows naturally.

2. HOW DID YOU PROCESS YOUR CALL?

Amazing women of influence surrounded me and helped me process my call to start a nonprofit. My mom, Dr. Marie Itiowe, ministered to the underprivileged in rural areas and she desired to expand her influence. On going to Bangor University in the UK for my MBA, I was blessed to meet Pastor Pauline of Assemblies of God Bangor. She was the first female pastor I had served with, and it was a blessing to learn from her how to courageously lead in a male-dominated ministry to make a difference. She ran Annie's Orphans charity shop, using proceeds for missions. Inspired by my mom's similar vision, I volunteered over 120 hours there while studying abroad and juggling three jobs. I was joyful to be making a difference, using God-given skills from my entrepreneurial activities as a law student.

This experience, combined with the financial challenges of missions growing up, inspired me to create a self-sustaining ministry. In the UK, I also met remarkable women like our eighty-year-old missions leader and grandmothers doing great things for Jesus. They taught me that age is no restriction when following God, who uses both the old and the young, women and girls alike.

3. WHO HELPED YOU DISCERN YOUR CALL?

Various formal events and informal experiences helped me discern my call as I rubbed shoulders with others. While doing my MBA in the UK, I traveled to Indonesia to attend the Lausanne Movement's Younger Leaders Gathering (YLG), which affirmed my leadership potential, catalyzing my growth toward my call. Despite being younger than the minimum age requirement, my years of service in campus ministry and teen ministry helped me get selected.

During the YLG congress, a pivotal moment occurred during a presentation on the world's hunger and poverty index, which included a practical demonstration of a "poverty meal." The organizers served all attendees a dinner consisting of white rice, corn, and a hint of carrot in water. This meal was intended to show how little some impoverished people had to eat, but it left some participants disgruntled.

Later that night, participants bought food from the streets of Jakarta. Hearing someone say, "They could have called for an offering for the poor instead of subjecting us to such a meal" saddened me. Praying on how God would have me respond to the exercise's purpose unexpectedly led to the birth of GIFT, a nonprofit aimed at addressing poverty and hunger through agriculture, skills training, and community development. The vision of GIFT fused my ministerial experiences and fund-providing business strategies garnered from the work at the charity shop with my training as a lawyer.

Graduating with distinction from my MBA program in the UK, I faced a pivotal decision: stay in the UK with its higher standard of living or return to Nigeria. Seeking God's guidance, I saw that the opportunities involved in staying were not in alignment with the visions God placed in my heart and in this way, I discerned his leading to return home and I began packing my bags.

I recognized some of God's wisdom in this leading when, after my return to Nigeria, my connections from a European Youth Ministry Leaders Conference in Spain led to generous donations of thousands of Bibles, which we distribute to this day as of the time of this writing on mission trips and to new converts.

During the COVID-19 pandemic, God spoke to me through a vision, which is one of the ways I have learned to hear his voice. In this vision, I encountered a little girl in critical need but lacked sufficient resources to help her. I sought help from others who provided what she needed, and I delivered it to her.

This vision spurred me to start a fundraiser to assist vulnerable people in my community and beyond struggling to feed their families due to the pandemic's economic impact. Encouraged by friends and family and convinced it was God's plan, we launched the fundraiser through GIFT, our now-registered nonprofit. Despite initial doubts, we saw the Lord use this challenging season to catalyze positive transformation as we responded to him and provided thousands of meals to hundreds of families and preached the gospel in various cities.

4. WHAT GIVES YOU JOY AND WHAT'S MOST CHALLENGING IN YOUR WORK?

Witnessing marks of transformation such as seeing plants grow, smiles, and hope in people's eyes when their needs are met makes me joyful. Being considered a vessel whom God can use to facilitate this transformation is incredibly fulfilling.

One such profound moment occurred when a woman received eye treatment and glasses during an outreach two days after my wedding ceremonies. Her exclamation, "Now I can read my Bible!" encapsulates the impact we can have on people's lives, making all the challenges encountered along the way worthwhile. Above all, there's deep satisfaction in being obedient to God's call. Knowing that I am aligned with his will and that my work pleases him brings me immense joy and fulfillment.

However, running a startup nonprofit without grants has its challenges. When you are established in a country with many scammers who use ministry fronts, it takes more effort to prove that you are different, so convincing potential supporters to join our cause can be an uphill climb. Emotionally, raising funds for each project and spending personal resources to fill the gaps can be daunting.

Finding the right team members has been another challenge, but I have seen the power of clearly communicating the vision: "Write down the revelation and make it plain," as God instructed Habakkuk to do (Habakkuk 2:2, NIV), and trust God to bring the right people to "run with it."

5. WHAT ADVICE DO YOU WISH SOMEONE HAD GIVEN YOU ABOUT YOUR CALL/MINISTRY?

It took almost two years before the Lord finally opened the door for me to go to Gordon-Conwell Theological Seminary (GCTS). However, when this door opened, it was a life-transforming experience I remain grateful to God for. From GCTS and through my time in the United States, I was able to carry out multiple impact-filled mission projects valued at several thousand dollars that led to the salvation of souls and community transformation.

At that point, though, I wish that someone had told me that following God involves several uncertainties. In my situation, uncertainty stemmed from running a nonprofit ministry as a single African woman in a patriarchal society that tends to place minimal value on single women. It was going to be challenging, making the prospect of meeting the organization's goals seem less likely. I wish someone had told me that I would need a lot of patience and perseverance before winning. I wish someone had told me that God's timing even for God's things depended solely on him. While I was not told these things and felt unprepared for them as a result, the Lord used my life experiences to teach me while shaping my story and relationship with him through it all.

A call from the Lord always involves our personal lives, too, which can be riddled with painful circumstances. Not long after I arrived at seminary, I was invited to speak at a "messiology" seminar. I had all the nice-to-say things outlined until my friend pointed out that I needed to focus on the mess in my story. I needed to share with fellow believers how the Lord helped my family through a season of grieving multiple losses. How my mom, Marie, my sister, Glory, my church-given elder sister, Ebere, and Dennis, who was driving the car, were all killed in a crash in one day. How the three women I had looked up to and grown up with in my home were dead. Now I needed to step up and grow up, be there for my dad, Pastor Alfred, and be the big sister at home to my younger sisters, Goodness and Gladden (my eldest sister Grace was married and out of the country at the time).

No one prepared me to cover the big roles those three women had filled, yet everyone expected me, a young lady just out of her teens, to have the answers. No one told me we could be serving God yet encounter such tragedy. It would have been easy for me to become bitter and cynical and walk away from God. However, I showed that I was in fact saved through Christ when God gave me peace and comfort as I was reminded of the hope I have of being reunited with my family members in eternity, since they were all born again.

My "messiology" message includes several broken marriage engagements, health challenges, disappointment from potential donors, limiting government policies, and many more situations that no one prepares you for. Yet I have seen God remain faithful as I have followed him through each season, and all I was not told has made me stronger.

In following God, the role of family, friends, pastors, and mentors is crucial. Find people who will believe in you enough to invest in you and give you space to rise and shatter glass ceilings. Throughout my ongoing journey, deep connections with godly friends and the support of such networks have been pillars of strength and growth through various seasons. The bonds I have with my remaining siblings and their families have flourished; we have welcomed a new mother, Dr. Akachi, and three new brothers—Ekene, Gugua, and Obioma.

My time in seminary and in the United States ended with a difficult decision. There was a nudge in my spirit to go home to Nigeria, but I struggled with it due to the pressures to stay in the United States. I sought counsel from mentors who prayerfully affirmed what I was sensing. Still struggling after receiving their feedback, I pled for divine guidance, asking for more signs. Soon after, my support systems in the United States started to break down and at this point it was all the indication I needed, and I obeyed. The decision to return to Nigeria, which seemed foolish to many, showed God's infinite wisdom as it led to our nonprofit securing a land grant of over one hundred acres, to my marriage to my sweetheart, Joseph—a miracle I didn't expect so soon after my return—as well as to multiple grand ministerial and business opportunities.

I am in hopeful anticipation of where he will lead us next. And I have learned that through the twists and turns, as we remain grounded in his word it will be a lamp to our feet and a light to our path. While we may not know what lies ahead, as we prayerfully keep trusting in him to birth those great visions by the help of his Spirit, we are assured that his presence will go with us, and he will give us rest.

21
NONPROFITS
Ahmi Lee

Ahmi Lee is a preacher, speaker, and consultant for churches and nonprofits. She is the author of *Preaching God's Grand Drama* and a board member of Redeemer City to City.

1. HOW DID YOU GET INTERESTED IN YOUR FIELD/MINISTRY?

I never thought I would be a preacher or theologian or be in the nonprofit sector, let alone that I would be simultaneously wearing different hats in my vocation. I first sensed God's call on my life in fifth grade. I was born into a Christian home, but earlier that fifth-grade year I committed to making the faith passed down to me my own. A spiritual growth spurt followed, accompanied by a ferocious hunger to learn more about Jesus. I read pages and pages of scripture every day and attended every worship service offered by my Korean church.

One Friday night, I was at the weekly late-night prayer gathering with my mom. Following the sermon, it was our church's tradition to scatter in the dimmed sanctuary, each person finding a spot to pray for as long as they wanted. Like warriors gearing up for a war, as soon as the service was over, everyone moved with purposefulness and anticipation to their usual places. By then, I had my favorite place, next to the large windows, several feet behind my mom who camped out by a pillar. It was there next to the big windows overlooking a dark cemetery that I first came to understand God's love and compassion for the broken world and felt my heart swell and ache. I prayed, "Lord, I'm small and weak. But if I can do something, please use me." My prayer that night was not so much a response to a specific vocation or agenda of God I sensed for my life, but rather a heartfelt alignment of myself with God's purpose to spread Christ's life and hope in this world, whatever form that might take in my life.

When it comes to vocation, some people know the one special thing they want to do and find fulfillment in dedicating much of their lives to it. Others may be more like me, a hyphenated person energized by engaging in multiple pursuits and integrating the disparate parts. As a Korean-Japanese American, my background and identity are tricultural. I was educated and formed in the global context of an international school in Japan where students from sixty-some countries gathered to learn. My interests and passions have been equally diverse and multifaceted from a young age.

At times I have felt confused and fragmented about my identity and belonging. Navigating boundary crossings has not always been enjoyable either. Yet God has used everything in my life to cultivate and fortify a sense of curiosity and openness to new experiences, and to drive me to learn and thrive across domains, no matter where the journey takes me. And it has indeed taken me to unforeseen places. What has endured over the years, however, is my childhood prayer that the Holy Spirit has kept alive in me, a prayer that I want to keep living out in new ways. I learned early on that the world is a big place, and if I abide in Christ, wherever I pitch my tent is *Bethel* (a dwelling place of God). The ground I stand on matters, but I have come to understand that *I* matter to God—and the *world* matters to God—and "surely the LORD is in this place" (Genesis 28:16, NIV).

2. HOW DID YOU PROCESS YOUR CALL?

When I offered myself to serve God vocationally, I had a strong sense of urgency, joy, and peace that I had not felt about anything else. In the years that followed, my family and church community played a huge role in helping me to discern and understand the significance of my commitment. God also used my time studying his word to clarify my motives and thoughts and allowed my faith community and me to identify and affirm my gifts through different life experiences.

One such formative experience was getting involved in street evangelism. Shortly after I responded to God's call on my life, my church befriended a nearby Japanese Baptist church that did street evangelism every Saturday evening. My brother and I joined them that year—and we didn't miss a week (except when we got sick) until we both graduated from high school and moved away from Japan. In the early years, about twenty of us—pastors, college students, young adults, and a couple of younger ones like me—gathered outside a bustling downtown train station. Standing next to street musicians, palm readers, and male bar hosts wearing sleek black suits, we sang praise songs, passed out tracts to passersby, and took turns preaching a short gospel message with a megaphone to people and cars waiting for a green light at a busy intersection (this later became my first preaching training ground!).

Some of us talked with people who had questions or showed interest. As the years went by, the group dwindled in size. Some members got married and left. Life simply got too busy for others. Eventually, the only ones left in the group were my brother and me. I admit that we thought about quitting too. But each time we did, our parents reminded us of our decisions to follow where God leads. It's not that God demanded this specific service from us: We simply felt compelled to keep showing up at the post we believed God had placed us in for that season. This experience made me realize that serving God vocationally wasn't a distant aspiration, but that every life stage presents opportunities to show up for God and demonstrate my love and commitment to Jesus.

Given my love for scripture, it's not surprising that my path led me to pursue my MDiv at Trinity Evangelical Divinity School and my PhD in theology and preaching at Fuller Theological Seminary, and eventually to teach at my doctoral alma mater. My journey through those years had its share of hardships, but with each step I experienced greater clarity and joy in my calling (even if it entails heartaches too). About the time that COVID-19 was peaking, I sensed God opening a door to a new adventure. At the time, I was elbow-deep in my faculty role, diligently carving out my academic career.

I suppose the *apokalypsis* (revelation) of the global pandemic reordered my priorities and put me in touch with my deep longing to venture out of the ivory tower of the seminary to be "on the ground" with everyday people. I realized I wanted to interface more directly with real-world problems that have a tangible and more immediate impact on people's lives. So, I stepped into the world of nonprofits, keeping a foothold in academia. I went from professor of preaching at Fuller to chief partnership officer at a Christian nonprofit. I didn't know what that vocational path would look like, but I sensed it would be at the intersection of the church, academia, and the public sphere.

In a way, even now I continue to process my calling because my story continues to be written. Still, I can look back with confidence, assured that I've been guided this far by the prayers and support of my family, friends, and faith communities and by the formative experiences God has allowed in my life. Through it all, I see clearly that I'm a child who offered up five loaves and two fish, and God has shown up in my life way more than I ever have for him.

3. WHO HELPED YOU DISCERN YOUR CALL?

My mom was the most significant influence in my childhood in discerning my calling. My parents aren't perfect, but I know they did their best to model the life of a Christian disciple in their flawed but sincere ways. My mom was the loudest voice that cheered me on and pushed me to follow God's leading in my life.

As an adult, my husband became my best friend, advocate, and partner in life and ministry who gives me the courage to step into places of need if God is calling me there. I am also indebted to loving mentors, friends, and colleagues who have walked with me in my high and low points. They were critical to shaping my imagination to see God's promises being fulfilled in my life—even when I couldn't. Although I've been generally blessed with people who believed that God had gifted and called me for ministry, I've also encountered critics along my way. The pain inflicted by their words and looks (or averted gazes) lingers, but even those people played a role in refining my understanding of God, the church, the world, and myself.

4. WHAT GIVES YOU JOY AND WHAT'S MOST CHALLENGING IN YOUR WORK?

My greatest joy and challenge of my work in this season is navigating my various roles as a preacher, homiletic theologian, and nonprofit leader. I love the freedom and creativity that this space affords me, but juggling the different demands of my roles while striving to integrate them in a meaningful way is hard. I am learning the importance of flexibility, adaptability, and innovation this season. Also, pursuing a healthy work-life balance and a sense of well-being has now become a priority for me.

5. WHAT ADVICE DO YOU WISH SOMEONE HAD GIVEN YOU ABOUT YOUR CALL/MINISTRY?

I would have loved to have been reminded never to lose sight of joy. There were moments when I was so anxious about doing the "right thing" that I became adept at being dutiful but lost delight and a sense of wonder about life. I wanted to fit my life into a neat box. There was no fulfillment in that. Life is messy, unpredictable, and disruptive. This doesn't mean that joy is out of reach. Bearing our crosses and following the Lord may involve shedding blood and tears, yet it does not preclude experiencing genuine joy amidst the anguish and sorrow. It was for "the joy set before him" that Jesus "endured the cross, scorning its shame, and sat down at the right hand of the throne of God" (Hebrews 12:2, NIV).

It seems to me that Christian joy has a peculiar quality, one that is not the total opposite of grief and suffering. It is different from happiness or levity. It feels sacred and defies simple categorization. It's not something one conjures for oneself, but something that one receives. Joy is like a signpost within us that points to something good ahead, and we can be glad and hopeful about *that* reality. To have been reminded about the kind of joy that sustains us in our calling is a gift I wish someone had given me early in my life, call, and ministry.

22
POLITICS
Kaitlyn Schiess

Kaitlyn Schiess is a ThD student in Christian ethics at Duke Divinity School. She is the author of *The Ballot and the Bible* and *The Liturgy of Politics* and cohosts the "Holy Post" podcast.

1. HOW DID YOU GET INTERESTED IN YOUR FIELD/MINISTRY?

No career counselor advised me to spend my life talking about religion and politics—the two things you are *not* supposed to talk about in polite company. From one perspective, I stumbled my way into my work largely by accident. From the perspective of faith, God in his great mercy led me to work I never would have chosen and could not have expected. Like many people, I found my way into my work somewhat by accident. Like many women, I felt myself guided by God into work that I never anticipated—and faced many barriers I would have rather avoided.

2. HOW DID YOU PROCESS YOUR CALL?

I spent much of my childhood interested in politics and law. I went to college planning on attending law school, and the bulk of my undergraduate experience was filled with policy debate:

practice, research, traveling for tournaments. I loved competitive debate because it combined many other things I loved: research and reading, constructing airtight arguments, and speaking in front of other people. A career in law or politics seemed natural, and I was drawn to the idea of spending years in school reading and arguing with other people about important ideas.

I attended a very politically involved college, Liberty University. Liberty was founded by Jerry Falwell Sr., an important figure in the Christian political movement known as the Moral Majority. While the school had always maintained connections to conservative politics, in the years I was at Liberty, Jerry Falwell Sr.'s son Jerry Falwell Jr. became deeply involved in the 2016 election. Politicians and pundits spoke on campus regularly, reporters interviewed students about their thoughts on the visiting candidates, and our campus was regularly covered in national media outlets. Often, these candidates would speak in "convocation," our thrice-weekly version of chapel. This meant that thousands of Liberty students would gather in an arena to sing worship songs and pray before hearing from a candidate for elected office. This combination of worship and politics led me to ask theological questions I had never asked before: What is the role of the church in political life? How should the Bible shape a Christian's politics? Is there something about our political life that inspires or demands worship that only God is owed?

At the same time as I was becoming more intimately exposed to questions about Christianity and politics, I was increasingly reconsidering a career in law. A church I had attended as a child was in desperate need of volunteers for a youth camp over the summer, and my mom was on the church staff, so I was an easy target. Although spending a week in a cabin with middle school girls sounded like a particularly frightening nightmare, I was cajoled into volunteering.

That week changed my life. I not only discovered that I loved talking about the Bible and praying with these girls, but I also had a powerful encounter with the God who is not the least bit impressed with my measures of success. For an overachieving, anxious twenty-year-old, this encounter of complete and total grace was stunning. I remember sitting on the bus on the way home, watching the camp fade into the distance and thinking, "Nothing is ever going to be the same again."

3. WHO HELPED YOU DISCERN YOUR CALL?

I decided to apply to seminary instead of law school, a decision that felt so terrifying I did not tell anyone about it for many months. I agonized over whether this was a reckless and silly choice, motivated by the spiritual rush of a week of camp rather than a genuine calling from God. Then one day, as I paced the hallways near my on-campus job, anxiously weighing my future in my mind, I thought to myself, "If I just knew everything was going to be okay, I'd go to seminary." Immediately, the Holy Spirit convicted me. *If I knew everything was going to be okay? Did I not have faith in the God who had taken care of me my whole life? Did I not trust that God had a plan I might not yet understand?* I decided I was going to seminary.

When I arrived at seminary, I was convinced I had chosen the holier path. "I used to be caught up in the worldly details of politics," I thought, "but I have chosen the better thing." I confidently decided that "politics has nothing to do with the church or theology." Then I watched as the ongoing 2016 election wreaked havoc in the churches around me: dividing congregations, sowing fear and anger among faithful people, tempting leaders towards all kinds of political idolatry. I quickly realized that politics was affecting the church whether we liked it or not.

I also realized that many of my peers—students preparing for pastoral ministry—knew that the church had some role to play in the political arena, but were entirely ill equipped for navigating it. The churches they were preparing to serve were often either captivated by political idolatry or too terrified and exhausted by politics to engage in it faithfully. Through conversations with friends and professors, I began to see a role for myself in helping churches and church leaders navigate the political world.

I realized that not only was I well equipped for this work—I had a background in political theory, I had studied American political history, I had spent years in debate keeping up with the minutiae of American politics—but I was hungry to learn what resources the Christian tradition already had for addressing political dysfunction. As I studied—in my seminary classes and in my personal study—I learned that not only did the church have incredible resources for faithful political life, but the strict separation I thought existed between politics and faith was nonexistent.

In seminary I discovered political theology, the area of Christian theology that considers how humans should live together in communities. I also discovered a crucial theological truth: that Scripture is not merely about my personal spiritual life but instead tells a grand, cosmic story about God creating and redeeming all of creation. That story does not just involve individual people but is centrally interested in the flourishing of human *communities*. I discovered that the call God gave in the beginning of the story—to rule and reign over creation, to take the good gifts of creation and make something good with them (Genesis 1:27–31)—was never revoked. My discovery of political theology was not merely the discovery of a new field of theology, it was the discovery that God cares about much more than our souls—he cares about our bodies, our communities, the creation we inhabit, and the boring details of how we get along with one another.

4. WHAT GIVES YOU JOY AND WHAT'S MOST CHALLENGING IN YOUR WORK?

Near the beginning of my theological education, I was captivated by a theology that made politics *matter*—not because it was fun to argue about, not because God was on one political "side" or the other, but because people and the communities we create matter to God. In a way, this theology drew me right back to where I started—passionate about politics—but in another sense, it opened an entirely different world to me. Politics was no longer a separate sphere of life with its own rules and standards of success, it was an important aspect of human life—and remained under the gracious rule of Christ. Politics was both demoted and elevated: demoted from its place as a source of identity and community, and elevated as another sphere in which Christians can faithfully labor, attentive to the work of the Holy Spirit and expectant that God will work in surprising ways.

I have spent the last five years working on issues of theology and politics: studying, writing, speaking, podcasting, and teaching. I love speaking at churches or universities and witnessing the exact moment that someone starts to understand this bigger story of Scripture. After I preached at a church recently, a woman came up to me and said, "When I saw that you were talking about politics, I wanted to run out the back door, but I was sitting in the front row, so I couldn't. But now I'm so glad I couldn't get out of there, because you opened my eyes to why politics matters to God." I have no desire to convince people to vote in a certain way. I want people to understand that our whole lives, including our political lives, matter to God. I want people in desperate and vulnerable situations to know that God has spoken against their exploitation and abuse. I want people in power to know that God has spoken about how they should use their power. I want people searching for resources about how to live well in diverse communities to know that God has spoken about how communities can best flourish. I want people in the pews of churches to expect that when the pages of the Bible are opened, the words we read will say something to both our personal spiritual lives *and* our public political lives.

Perhaps the best thing I get to do is spend time with women college or seminary students discerning their own calls—to ministry, to law, to public service. I love hearing them wrestle with how God might be leading them and helping them recognize their next steps.

I often tell them that when I was in college, I could not have imagined the life I have now and the work I am doing. I walked into every step of my journey not entirely sure what was next—into college, from college to seminary, from seminary to my doctoral program—and God provided clarity along the way. God led me to work that I thought was not "spiritual" or "holy" enough, teaching me that all work done by the power of the Spirit to bring goodness, justice, and flourishing to human communities is holy work.

5. WHAT ADVICE DO YOU WISH SOMEONE HAD GIVEN YOU ABOUT YOUR CALL/MINISTRY?

My first week of seminary, I remember feeling jealous of the people (usually men) who seemed so naturally confident in their callings. They not only felt comfortable in theological education, but they also felt certain God was calling them to pastoral ministry—and no one questioned what they were "going to do with" their degrees. Now I am strangely thankful for my uncertainty and doubt. They kept me curious, openhanded, and dependent upon God. I was able to see new paths forward because I was not overly certain about a single path.

As you discern your calling, remember this: God is preparing places for you that you cannot picture right now. He is the God who is "able to do immeasurably more than all we ask or imagine" (Ephesians 3:20, NIV). When it seems like the political world is too dark for anything good to happen, remember that God works in the places we do not expect and through the unlikeliest of people. The political world is not devoid of God's presence or action, despite its great challenges. When God's people are willing to humbly enter it, aware of the allure of power and the temptation of various idolatries, we can find that the Spirit is able to enliven and encourage us, providing the strength and compassion we need to seek justice, show mercy, and walk humbly with our God (Micah 6:8).

23
PUBLISHING
Bunmi Ishola

Bunmi Ishola works as a senior editor, focusing on children's books, for PRH Christian Publishing Group, a division of Penguin Random House.

1. HOW DID YOU GET INTERESTED IN YOUR FIELD/MINISTRY?

I've always been enamored with stories, even before I could read for myself. With my sisters, I'd playact elaborate plotlines and then I'd beg my eldest sister to type them out so the tales would never get lost. Once I could sound out letters and make sense of the words on a page for myself, it seemed I was never without a book in my hand. When my family moved from America to Nigeria (and later, back again), the stories remained my friends and constants, making sure I never felt lonely or out of place, and keeping me moored, even as other things kept shifting.

If you asked me as a very young child what I wanted to be, I would say I wanted to be Anne of Green Gables. And then once I realized I couldn't *become* a storybook character, I wanted to help create ones that would accompany readers through the ups and downs of life, much like my favorite characters did, and continue to do, for me. The world is a complex place, and stories have a way of helping simplify things: a way of illuminating an idea that feels murky, a way of reminding us we aren't alone, of revealing our shared humanity.

I knew that stories mattered—they bear witness to what is but can also expand our imagination of what could be—but I didn't start my career there. "Publishing" was a nebulous word and world. I couldn't articulate what type of jobs I'd want within it besides "author," and everyone I spoke to essentially said that I'd become a starving artist if I didn't have something more practical as a backup.

And so, I went to school for journalism. It was a different kind of storytelling but had many of the same components I was passionate about: every time I interviewed someone and wrote an article (or even an obituary!) I felt I was making space for people not only to share the stories they carried within, but to also share them with a wider audience.

But I didn't love the fast-paced environment. In journalism, yesterday's news was old news and no longer relevant. Newspapers and magazines got recycled and composted, their stories rarely returned to or cherished. I wanted something with a slower pace, something that allowed me to walk alongside people for longer periods, to help create something that was more enduring.

As I tried to figure out what was next, I fell into teaching—I had tutored kids throughout college, then substitute taught as a filler before and after grad school, and so when I left the journalism world, I found myself teaching middle school social studies. Even though I was teaching about government, economics, geography, and the like, I still leaned on storytelling to guide me. I'd scour fiction and nonfiction texts, looking for excerpts I could pull to help make abstract concepts more concrete or to serve as a "real-world" example of what I was teaching. As a behavior management tool (and, honestly, to get my mind ready for the day or transition between classes), I implemented a ten- to fifteen-minute silent reading time to begin each class period. And when I didn't know what to do when I discovered we had only thirty minutes of class on Wednesdays versus our usual fifty minutes . . . well, I was barely efficient enough to get through a whole lesson in fifty minutes, so I chose to use those short days as read-aloud days.

I knew stories were powerful from my own life, but it was a completely different experience to witness how impactful they were in the lives of my students: to hear the connections they'd make between what they read and what they were learning, the quality of the questions they would ask, the way they would empathize with each other and people worlds away from them. My experience teaching made even more clear the importance and need for stories to exist in the world.

So after seven years of teaching, when it felt clear that it was time to close that chapter, only one other job seemed to make sense to me. As an editor, I now have the honor of helping to shepherd stories into the world. And as a children's book editor, I recognize just how much more impact the books I edit can have. Those stories have the power to shape young minds, to influence the values and mindsets of the next generation.

2. HOW DID YOU PROCESS YOUR CALL?

I got fired from my very first "real" job (you know, the full-time, comes-with-benefits kind). I still remember getting into my car in the middle of the day, after being made to clear out my desk and being walked out. I started to drive home, but eventually had to pull over because I could no longer see through the tears and my body wracked with sobs. *This was it*, I thought, *I will forever bear this mark; I am ruined.*

Once I was able to breathe again, I called my parents, who were visiting from Nigeria and were currently with my eldest sister. I was supposed to fly out to join them in just a few days. The tears started flowing anew as I told them what had happened. I don't remember a whole lot about the conversation, except for one piece.

"You know Jeremiah 29:11?" my sister asked.

"For I know the plans I have for you," I responded.

"Yes, which is a truth you should hold on to, but I actually want you to read earlier in that chapter," she said. "The Israelites are in exile—life isn't at all how they would have envisioned it—but verse 7 says this: 'But seek the welfare of the city where I have sent you into exile, and pray to the Lord on its behalf, for in its welfare you will find your welfare.' Right now, being unemployed feels like you've been exiled, but I want you to find ways you can still add value to the people around you. No matter what comes after this, you can seek the welfare of that place, and from there you'll see God will take care of you."

That conversation was a turning point for me. And I still refer back to Jeremiah 29:7 whenever I'm feeling frustrated, confused, or purposeless about work and my career.

3. WHO HELPED YOU DISCERN YOUR CALL?

My sister shared that verse to encourage me when I was at my lowest point, when I thought that I had screwed up my "calling" and would have nothing to offer a future employer. Her sharing of that verse helped me reframe things: My calling is always first and foremost to seek the welfare of the "city." As Christians, we believe that this earth is not our final home. In some ways, we are all in constant exile. But if I choose to seek the welfare of whatever job I had, in whatever city I lived, whatever relationships I'm in, then I'm walking out God's purpose for me. *That's* my calling.

Right now, I get to seek the welfare of the children's publishing world. As an editor, I get to work on stories that I pray bring flourishing and speak life into the lives of young readers. But before I was an editor, I looked to "seek the welfare" of the tutoring center where I worked with students with learning disabilities. I made sure to "seek the welfare" at the YMCA, where I played with babies and wiped their butts while their parents worked out. I continued to "seek the welfare" over the six years I taught middle school.

I hope to continue to "seek the welfare" as a children's book editor until I retire, but even if I shift jobs, my calling won't change. I will always "seek the welfare" in whatever role God places me.

4. WHAT GIVES YOU JOY AND WHAT'S MOST CHALLENGING IN YOUR WORK?

I love that I get to read for a living! But I truly love getting to sit with authors and help them develop and clarify their ideas, making sure they're communicating their vision effectively. Much like when I was a teacher, I feel like I get to wear many hats: I also get to be my authors' counselor and advisor, one of their biggest champions and cheerleaders. I don't take for granted that they are trusting me with a piece of their hearts, and that is a great privilege and honor. I also enjoy seeing readers interact with the final book—knowing they loved a story and were impacted by it is such a delight. I get giddy whenever I see a positive review or see people sharing about a book I worked on (and beware if you ever run into me in a bookstore and you happen to even *look* at a book I edited!). Knowing how much books can change lives, I don't think I'll ever stop being in awe of the small part I play in putting one out in the world.

One challenge is that at the end of the day, I work for a business and not a ministry. I may *see* my work as a form of ministry, but the job itself is not. We are not giving out books for free; we make books for a profit. This is especially challenging since I work in the Christian publishing space where intrinsically we see every book we create as an opportunity to live out and share the gospel. It's a hard tightrope to walk, and at times one can feel a bit cynical when you lose a book at an auction because another publisher could pay more, or you can't reach the intended audience because advertising costs a lot, or you must pass on a book idea that you know holds needed truth, but you unfortunately can't justify the cost of acquiring it.

5. WHAT ADVICE DO YOU WISH SOMEONE HAD GIVEN YOU ABOUT YOUR CALL/MINISTRY?

Even with my sister pointing me to Jeremiah 29:7, it still took a lot of years for me to not feel anxious about whether I was "living out my calling." The philosophy I described above took many years to form and really believe. So, one piece of advice that I give to people now, and that I wish had been given to me, is to remember that your calling is not about *what* you do. It's about *why* you do it and for *whom* you do it. If I approach my work with the goal to love God and love others, to glorify him and make his name known, then I'm living out my calling. I may not do it perfectly, but if that's where my heart is focused, then I have nothing to worry about except staying the course.

IV
Calling in Academic Ministry

24
TEACHING COMMUNICATION

Arianna Molloy

Arianna Molloy is Associate Professor of Organizational Communication at Biola University. She is the author of *Healthy Calling: From Toxic Burnout to Sustainable Work.*

1. HOW DID YOU GET INTERESTED IN YOUR FIELD/MINISTRY?

I changed my major five times in college.

Choosing a major designed to carve out the trajectory of my career, and ultimately impact the quality of my adulthood, was more than daunting. It felt paralyzing.

In wrestling with this, I began to realize my communication classes didn't feel like drudgery or simply an educational checklist. They felt like light bulb moments, like developing superpowers for new ways of seeing and hearing. It was a year-long process for me to recognize that choosing a major I loved, even if I wasn't sure what I'd do with it, wasn't the easy way out: it was the wise way forward.

Did you know people change jobs approximately ten times between the ages of eighteen and forty-two?[1] The tools and

---

[1] J. M. Berg, A. M. Grant, and V. Johnson, "When Callings Are Calling: Crafting Work and Leisure in Pursuit of Unanswered Occupational Callings," *Organization Science* 21 (2010): 973–94.

strategies we learn in our majors are often more important than the label of our major. The key is developing skill sets and passions that can be applied to several occupational contexts. I chose communication, or it chose me. I'm still not sure. The interactions and layered messages I used to take for granted, what I noticed—upon entering a room, in a formal meeting, during a speaking event, in a written message, on a Netflix show, among family, friends, or work colleagues—not everyone noticed. So I took the vulnerable leap of trusting what I sensed God was developing in me, not realizing it would unfold into a work calling.

2. HOW DID YOU PROCESS YOUR CALL?

I remember the exact spot I was driving on the Southern California freeway near Anaheim when a sudden pop and colorful burst of Disney fireworks softened the ding of an email notification on my phone. It was a new bank payment alert for the job I recently took as a full-time, tenure-track professor. "Oh yeah," I thought, "I'm getting paid to do this . . . but I'd do it for free." (I mean, maybe not the mountainous piles of grading). With a belly chuckle, I realized I was living out a work calling.

The irony is, in my doctoral program, I began studying what is now my research area, communication about meaningful work and calling. I'm fascinated by the significant impact of work perceptions on motivation, satisfaction, resilience, and well-being, as well as workaholism, job idolization, and burnout.[2] Yet, for a long time, I somehow thought my own sense of calling was only felt in personal relationships. I liked work. I didn't know I could love work.

Here's what I know now: work calling is inherently about relationship—with the Caller, the called, and the community.

---

2   K. Arianna Molloy and Christina R. Foust, "Work Calling: Exploring the Communicative Intersections of Meaningful Work and Organizational Spirituality," *Journal of Communication Studies* 67, no. 3 (2016): 1–20, https://doi.org/10.1080/10510974.2016.1148751; B. J. Dik and R. D. Duffy, *Make Your Job a Calling* (West Conshohocken, Pa.: Templeton, 2012).

We cannot fully process calling without acknowledging these dynamics.

3. WHO HELPED YOU DISCERN YOUR CALL?

If you were to imagine two people, one a wise and faithful Gary Cooper or Jimmy Stewart type of cowboy and the other a combination of Disney's Mary Poppins plus Maria von Trapp (from *The Sound of Music*), they would exemplify my dad and mom.

Not everyone gets to be raised by supportive parents—I realize it's a huge privilege. However, I know the love of God because of my parents, and I know what support feels like because of them. From a very young age, they included me in conversations about work and life. They valued my opinion. I felt seen, heard, and safe with them—fertile soil for cultivating a calling.

Unfortunately, there were some educators in my life who left scars from poor teaching and lack of empathy. Or even a few friends who believed they were helping by telling me to dream smaller. On the other hand, there have also been professors who let me ask questions and gave me space to wrestle with ideas, mentors who offered me opportunities to learn and grow, and friends who reminded me I was not alone in this journey, even if I couldn't see more than two steps ahead.

As an adult, knowing that calling is a dynamic and ongoing process, I am especially grateful to be married to a man who fully supports my dreams and goals, often encouraging me to keep a growth mindset.

I think the main takeaway is that a healthy calling is rooted in community, and we must be careful who our community includes.

4. WHAT GIVES YOU JOY AND WHAT'S MOST CHALLENGING IN YOUR WORK?

Two of my core passions are mentorship and collaborative learning. I love being able to mentor students. I love encouraging them in their development, helping them feel seen, heard, and valued. I love watching the spark of their own light bulb moments, offering spaces for them to wrestle with concepts resulting in greater wisdom and discernment. And it feels almost effortless to teach them communication theories and practical applications that help make professional and personal spaces better.

Two of my core convictions are apprenticeship to Jesus[3] and a growth mindset. It gives me a holy kind of gladness to help people have real encounters with Jesus, where they not only choose to believe in him as Lord but also recognize the great need of following him in all they do. It gives me joy to offer every student the opportunity to surprise themselves—in discovering how smart they are, how big an impact they can make, and how capable they are of experiencing success when they don't give up.

Whether it's in a college classroom, a consulting experience, or speaking event, when I have the honor of talking about the Lord as the great communicator, as our faithful and loving caller, as the one who is both majestic king and lover of our souls, this is joy upon joy upon joy. It is holy elation.

What's often most challenging is the blurred line between my professional calling and workaholism or job idolatry. It's very easy to conflate feeling compelled to respond to the Caller with a compulsion to be consumed by the calling. It's unfortunately too easy to experience job creep—the sliding scale of saying "yes" too much, either because we want to or because we feel pressured to. We should never confuse the calling with the Caller. When these are out of order, we run the risk of burnout.

Ultimately, I feel passionate about helping others care for their callings with awe, delight, and accountability. To live out our callings is to live a life of worship to the Lord. When callings grow toxic, we put on unnecessary, rusted shackles and bind ourselves to burnout. I don't want that for anyone.

---

[3] See John Mark Comer, *Practicing the Way: Be with Jesus, Become Like Him, Do as He Did* (Colorado Springs, Colo.: Waterbrook, 2024).

5. WHAT ADVICE DO YOU WISH SOMEONE HAD GIVEN YOU ABOUT YOUR CALL/MINISTRY?

Choosing to pursue a calling can be lonely, so pursue mentors and community. There will be sacrifice, possibly job judgment, and seasons of great unknown. Lean in anyway. It's worth it.

Don't let graduate school break you. If you can, find a study buddy and/or writing pal. Find a hobby that will help you get out of your head and keep your heart soft. For me, it was hiking, reading for fun, cooking, and learning how to run half marathons.

Don't confuse having a bad day with not having a calling. On the best day, about 80 percent of what I do feels like a calling. There will always be elements of work that aren't meaningful or enjoyable.

Hold your calling with an open hand rather than a closed fist. The first is an act of vulnerable trust; the second is a dangerous attempt to control. Calling is about relationships; therefore, expect them to grow and change as you grow and change. Don't try to control it or it will turn from sweet manna to worm-infested rot (Exodus 16:20).

Never use your work calling as an excuse to harm or not show up for those the Lord has entrusted to you. Multiple and seasonal callings are more common than we realize. When I became a mom, I felt a whole different (and unexpected) calling as a mother that wasn't in conflict with my calling as a professor but did take some readjusting. For example, I had to get comfortable with modified work expectations and goals as I learned to co-parent and care for my son. I was intentional about saying "I *get to* go to work" versus "I *have to* go to work." I learned to be okay with responding to student emails a little later or having slightly fewer office hours so I could be present with my kid. Frankly, I'm still figuring this out. But I'm not confused about the order: God, spouse, kid, work.

Prioritize caring for your *relationship* with the caller—I truly believe a top value here is Sabbath. Diligently guard routine times of rest so you can slow down, breathe, reflect, and learn. If Sabbath rest has felt boring, take time to figure out why. It may be that an understanding of rest needs adjusting. For example, did you know there are seven types of rest?[4] Sabbath is the first thing God called holy in the Bible, and it's important we understand why.[5]

Lastly, as a woman in grad school and at the start of my career, I wish I wouldn't have felt like my work calling somehow eliminated me from having a family of my own—that's a lie. I remember being one of the last people in my friend group to get married. It was lonely. Sometimes I didn't know if my hope for a spouse was naive foolishness or a possible reality. When I was single, and a newly minted doctoral graduate, some well-meaning friends told me to limit "big words" on dates and not bring up the fact that I'm a professor. I'm embarrassed to say that, in my desire to "be open," I believed them for a short while. Then I met my husband (also an academic). Talking to him was fun and I never felt like I had to be smaller. He was confident in who he was and his goals, enough so that he shared space with me. I like him and I love him. He was worth the wait.

Don't give up. Don't give in. Choose routine rest. Seek healthy community. Stay humble. Be vulnerable. Be brave. You can do this!

[4]   Saundra Dalton Smith, "7 Types of Rest That Every Person Needs," *TED*, January 6, 2021, https://ideas.ted.com/the-7-types-of-rest-that-every-person-needs/.

[5]   Arianna Molloy, "Embracing the Liturgy of Labor Day," *Christianity Today*, September 1, 2022, https://www.christianitytoday.com/ct/2022/august-web-only/labor-day-anniversary-christian-work-culture-sabbath.html.

25
TEACHING ENGLISH/LITERATURE

Jessica Hooten Wilson

Jessica Hooten Wilson is the Fletcher Jones Chair of Great Books at Pepperdine University. She is the author and editor of nine books, including *Flannery O'Connor's "Why Do the Heathen Rage?"* and *Reading for the Love of God*.

1. HOW DID YOU GET INTERESTED IN YOUR FIELD/MINISTRY?

From the time I was four years old, I read everything I could find, though my primary fascination was with novels and poetry. I had a large desk in my office and a typewriter—hand-me-downs from a church office—where I would sit for hours and write newspaper articles, columns full of my opinions on sundry topics, and of course, stories and poems. But it was not until I discovered the stories of Flannery O'Connor that I began to see writing as a Christian vocation. As a teenager, I imitated her haunting works that were full of sin, grace, and holy freaks. In college, I read a book called *On Becoming a Novelist*, where the author John Gardner advised anyone who wanted to become a writer to first be an avid reader. This advice led me to graduate studies in literature and theology, and my desire has only increased to discover every day how God tells our story or how stories show us who God is.

2. HOW DID YOU PROCESS YOUR CALL?

When I was a junior in college, a small group of students heard from God that he wanted them to postpone graduation by a year and venture to China to be missionaries. After their announcement of this grand change of course, I left that church service in tears. *Why had God not called me?* As a child, I had played with the idea of being a nun (until I realized you were supposed to be Catholic, and I didn't want to wear black). I was very devout, probably overly pious, the kind of child that other kids mock as a Goody-Two-shoes, so God calling others to do his work felt like a smack in the face. But on the phone with my dad, I heard the greatest wisdom he could have shared with me in that moment: God had called me—he had called me to be a writer.

3. WHO HELPED YOU DISCERN YOUR CALL?

In addition to Flannery O'Connor and my father's guidance, there were lots of voices that pushed me towards a vocation in reading and writing, affirmative voices that became like a current I would have had to fight against to do any other work. People in my church would ask me to write poems for different seasons of the calendar, namely, Easter or Christmas. One teacher, newly hired at my high school, had heard of my great work as the school's newspaper editor and invited me to lunch during the summer at Jason's Deli. She wanted me to be the yearbook editor for my senior year, a post which I had never even considered. During college, I won enough scholarship money each year through writing contests to pay for my tuition. Other awards or moments of recognition added up and encouraged my vocation. I was selected to read a short story for the board of regents at their retreat, or I was offered an internship for *The Journal of Christianity and Literature*. Despite other setbacks or moments where my work was rejected, these events acted as guideposts that assured me of my calling.

4. WHAT GIVES YOU JOY AND WHAT'S MOST CHALLENGING IN YOUR WORK?

Sometimes I draw on that line from *Chariots of Fire* where Eric Liddell says that he feels God's pleasure in him when he runs. For me, I feel that pleasure when I share what I'm reading, teach others to read, or spend time contemplating and writing. I especially love moments of epiphany when a scandalous text becomes clearer, or an idea becomes real in the words on the blank page.

I'm not sure that my work is as challenging as the things that surround my work. First, the digital age is annoying, constantly hammering for our attention, convincing us that we will only have our work read if we spend the time sharing it online. It's a tempting lie to fall for. Second, when you love what you do, it can be hard to prioritize the other realities to which God calls us: citizenship, service, even family life. I may adore my children, students, or friends, but I can also become so enamored with writing or reading that I must force myself to stop and spend time with those whom I love so much.

5. WHAT ADVICE DO YOU WISH SOMEONE HAD GIVEN YOU ABOUT YOUR CALL/MINISTRY?

People paraphrase Augustine as saying, "Love God and do what you want." That truth was something I could have heard earlier in my life. I sweated too much over doing what God wants and trying to hear exactly what that was—from how to spend my mornings, to what my major should be, to which job to accept, etc. If you love the Lord fully, you will do his will.

26
TEACHING ETHICS
Devan Stahl

Devan Stahl is Associate Professor of Religion at Baylor University and an adjunct associate professor at the Baylor College of Medicine. She is the author of *Disability's Challenge to Theology: Genes, Eugenics, and the Metaphysics of Modern Medicine.*

1. HOW DID YOU GET INTERESTED IN YOUR FIELD/MINISTRY?

If someone had told me as a teenager that I would become a professor of Christian ethics, I would have been delighted, but perhaps not surprised. What would have surprised me was the path that got me here. I was a pious evangelical youth group kid and school was just about the only thing I was good at. By sixteen I had read both volumes of John Calvin's *Institutes* and I was eager to learn as much theology as I could. Despite my eagerness, however, I was discouraged from seeing my calling as involving ministry. The church of my youth disallowed women from teaching adult men and ordination was out of the question. Such restrictions, however, never sat well with me. My mother was a lawyer for the US Army Judge Advocate General's Corps and was well acquainted with excelling in spaces dominated by men. If my mother could be deployed to a combat zone and help prosecute war criminals, why couldn't I be a pastor?

I brought these questions with me to college at the University of Virginia. I was not initially sure what I wanted to study, but I quickly fell in love with my religion classes. Whereas I had been told by my youth group pastors that there was little value in studying other religions and that the Bible could be clearly and simply read, I found myself awash in new and exciting theologies. I took classes in Judaism, Buddhism, Hinduism, and Islam, and I read feminist, liberation, and Black Christian theologians. The coherency of my belief system was shaken, but I never lost my faith. On the contrary, leaning into the complexities and tensions within Christian theology helped me see the liveliness of the tradition and learn the ways women like me had forged a path for themselves within patriarchal systems. I wasn't sure I wanted to be a minister, but it was becoming clear to me that there was nothing straightforward about denying all women the option.

After graduating from UVA, I went on to Vanderbilt Divinity School, the self-proclaimed "school of the prophets." Vanderbilt cultivated a community where students could become pastors, professors, or activists. I still wasn't sure which I wanted to be, but I was sure that VDS could help me in the discernment process.

Holding on to the piety of my youth, I assumed God "called" people to their vocation through a sort of intellectual telepathy. If I just prayed the right kind of prayer, God would implant a message in my mind telling me what I should do with my life. I never expected my call to come through my body, but at twenty-three I learned I was chronically ill, and my world came crashing down.

It began one morning in my feet. They were tingling and numb, the sort of sensation you get when your limbs fall asleep, but the feeling didn't go away. Instead, it spread up my legs, which made it difficult to walk. And then I was tired all the time. I began taking three- to four-hour naps in the afternoon and waking up in a groggy haze. Between my doctor appointments and my fatigue, school suddenly became very difficult, and I begged my teachers for more time and my administrators for more money. (I went to school before the Affordable Care Act and my student insurance stopped paying for any medical care just a couple months into the year.)

After months of medical testing, I was finally diagnosed with multiple sclerosis (MS) by a neurologist. He warned me I'd likely be in a wheelchair in five years. My future went from endless possibility to imminent dread. At Vanderbilt I had a diverse group of friends, but none of them were disabled, as far as I knew. Whereas I had multiple female role models, none of my faculty identified as disabled, and I couldn't remember anyone discussing disability as another embodied identity alongside sex and race.

Being chronically ill and disabled didn't initially feel like a calling: it felt like a burden, possibly even a tragedy. Barring some medical breakthrough, which didn't and doesn't seem likely, MS would not be something I could overcome. It would take a long time for me to realize the disability was a part of my calling.

2. HOW DID YOU PROCESS YOUR CALL?

Initially, I wasn't sure how to talk about my illness or who to talk about it with, so I began reading books. Nancy Mairs's honest and humorous spiritual autobiography about living with MS helped me to give voice to my fears and reimagine my hopes for the future. Nancy Eiesland's identity as a proud disabled Christian as well as her description of a disabled God shepherded me into a new discourse around disability pride and disability theology. Thomas Reynolds, Hans Reinders, John Swinton, and countless others helped me to see how my own theology had been shaped by various misconceptions regarding how bodies and minds should and should not function. My life was not tragic, it was typical. Most of us, if we live long enough, will experience disability. At a young age, I was already beginning to recognize my own vulnerability and mortality and the ways in which my theology had denied these aspects of my humanity. My disability, like my sex, became integral to how I understood myself and how I related to God.

3. WHO HELPED YOU DISCERN YOUR CALL?

Once the shock of my diagnosis had subsided and I found a new language for talking about disability, I was able to consider the future that God was calling me into. I had so many negative experiences with physicians and hospitals that chaplaincy seemed like a natural next step after divinity school. It was abundantly clear to me that while modern medicine had made incredible strides in curing and mitigating illness, physicians can sometimes be bad communicators and even worse spiritual care providers. Most do not have the time or skill to address the existential and spiritual suffering that can accompany illness. Hospital chaplains, on the other hand, are trained to have these hard conversations.

I began a Clinical Pastoral Education (CPE) residency in Nashville, Tennessee after graduating from Vanderbilt. My supervisor, David Nowlin, guided five residents through a year-long crash course in how to be present amid suffering. Chaplaincy training is trial by fire. Almost immediately, residents are sent to the hospital rooms of strangers, most of whom are experiencing the worst moment in their lives. No amount of classroom training can prepare you for these encounters. And while it was often heart-wrenching to hear patients' stories and to sit with them and their families as they died, it was clear to me that these spaces felt more comfortable than my church internship, where my empathy was rarely ignited in the same way.

What was difficult about CPE was not so much the death or suffering I witnessed, but the power hierarchies that devalued the work of chaplains and the institutional structures that made empathy and change difficult. Many of the clinicians I worked with seemed burnt out and distressed (crises that have become more pervasive since COVID). I could care for my colleagues, but I couldn't change the systems that left them feeling this way. I met someone in the hospital, however, who did have the power to change systems: the clinical ethicist.

Kate Payne was a force of nature. A legally trained former nurse, she carried a kind of moral authority and fortitude I had not witnessed before in the hospital. Up to that point I had never heard of a clinical ethicist, so I sought her out to learn all I could. As a full-time clinical ethicist, she responded to ethics consults by providing ethics recommendations and by mediating disputes between clinicians and patients. She also helped write hospital policies and she educated hospital staff on ethics issues. Her work inspired me to think about how I might help to change systems within health care.

Around that time, I also met another bioethicist working at Vanderbilt, Jeffrey Bishop, a physician with a PhD in philosophy who was teaching religion students how to think about the history and practice of modern medicine. Jeff was one of the first near strangers I told I had MS, and I rehearsed for him how my diagnosis had come to shape my theology. As I was wrapping up my CPE residency, Jeff was leaving Vanderbilt to serve as the director of the Albert Gnaegi Center for Health Care Ethics at Saint Louis University, and he encouraged me to apply to their doctoral program. I was already considering a doctoral degree in theology so that I could further explore disability and health care, but Jeff convinced me that the bioethics program at SLU would better serve my interests.

My educational training at Vanderbilt and my CPE residency prepared me well for my work at SLU, and upon graduation I landed a job at the Center for Ethics and Humanities in the Life Sciences (now the Center for Bioethics and Social Justice) in the College of Human Medicine at Michigan State University. Teaching medical students to be ethical care providers felt like a fitting way to live out my calling. My faculty appointment also allowed me to work as a clinical ethics consultant at our local hospitals. I not only had the satisfaction of teaching future doctors, but also of helping patients and clinicians as I witnessed Kate do years before.

Yet in a medical school I found it difficult to incorporate my theological training, so when Baylor University's religion department advertised a job in theological bioethics, I eagerly applied. At Baylor, I train premedical and prehealth students alongside religion students and graduate students in religion. I volunteer as a clinical ethicist at our local hospital, and I continue to educate medical trainees at all levels. At Baylor I feel that I can bring my whole self to my profession, which includes my intellectual training, embodied experiences, and spiritual identity.

4. WHAT GIVES YOU JOY AND WHAT'S MOST CHALLENGING IN YOUR WORK?

As a bioethicist, there are multiple and interconnected ways I can serve my community. As a teacher, I have the privilege of shaping the next generation of health care practitioners, many of whom will have their first exposure to clinical care by way of an ethics course. I am also drawing students' attention to disability ethics early on in their careers, before many of them will enter a helping profession or pastor a church. My work also affords me time to dwell deeply on my research, either through formulating foundational theories and practices in theological bioethics or participating in empirical research with interdisciplinary scholars in the humanities and sciences. Finally, my work as a clinical ethicist is a direct and tangible way for me to help people in my community using my knowledge of ethics and the health care system. This work in turn helps me to be a better teacher, because I am bringing real ethical dilemmas to my students, and inspires my research, which is often based on a challenge I encountered in the hospital.

The interdisciplinary nature of bioethics is both its strength and its challenge. I sometimes struggle to keep up with medical jargon in the clinic, to read enough theology and Christian ethics to converse with my colleagues in religion, or to keep pace with cutting-edge work in disability studies. And while I enjoy being in conversation with various faculty and clinicians across the profession, I often find myself spread thin. And because I deeply care about the subjects I teach and the work that I do, failure at any level can feel like failure to myself and the communities I am advocating for. Part of living into my calling is finding time for adequate rest and care and being gentle with myself when I don't live up to my own aspirations.

5. WHAT ADVICE DO YOU WISH SOMEONE HAD GIVEN YOU ABOUT YOUR CALL/MINISTRY?

Sometimes the best and most meaningful parts of your life are the things you did not choose, and you would not have chosen. Your calling is not a secret God whispers into your ear or a prize for your piety, but a path forged by the foreseen and unforeseen circumstances of your life. Many of those experiences will be painful, but there is no shortcut through them. Meaning is forged after years of struggle, consideration, and mentorship.

27
TEACHING NEW TESTAMENT
Madison N. Pierce

Madison N. Pierce is Associate Lecturer in New Testament at the University of St Andrews. She has written *Divine Discourse in the Epistle to the Hebrews* and is New Testament Editor at *Reviews of Biblical and Early Christian Studies.*

1. HOW DID YOU GET INTERESTED IN YOUR FIELD/MINISTRY?

My interest in teaching came much earlier than my interest in the New Testament. When I was in my first year of high school, I spent considerable time thinking about things that I enjoyed and wondering if they reflected ways that God had gifted me. During those times of discernment, I recognized that one thing that I really loved was teaching. Offering my peers analogies and explanations that helped them understand what we were reading together gave me so much joy. I also had a strong sense that I was not called to teaching generally but to teaching theology specifically. I felt so excited to commit to serving God vocationally, and I began to dream about how that would take shape.

But my excitement died when my mentors at the time learned about this. They told me that the Bible said that women could not teach anyone but other women and children, especially in the church. This was a new idea for me, but I trusted my spiritual leaders, and I accepted that I must have "misheard" God. (I knew that I was not called to women's or children's ministry.)

2. HOW DID YOU PROCESS YOUR CALL?

For the next five years, I struggled to find something that I loved nearly as much. In the meantime, when I went to college, I began as a music major. Leading music was a (moderately) acceptable role in the denomination I was in, and my church leaders steered me towards it. I could sing, and I enjoyed it; however, when I entered the program, I quickly saw the chasm between those truly gifted and me. I struggled to keep up, but I persisted.

I continued to persist until my second year of college when I became quite ill. My ability to sing was gone, effectively, and after months this did not seem to be something that would change anytime soon. And so, I switched to a Christian Studies major to continue a path towards leading music—whenever God restored my ability to do so. In the meantime, I intended to learn more about theology with the hope of teaching through the songs that I would select and maybe even write.

Nevertheless, this best-laid plan went awry in the very first week after I changed my major when I found myself in a course on the theology of Paul. Beginning on the first day, I felt something wake up in me that had been asleep for a long time—a passion to teach and to help others understand God. I saw the service of my professors and knew that seminary and a PhD were my path. My specific interest in New Testament came the next year. I simultaneously took Greek and a course on Hebrews and the Catholic Epistles. I fell in love with the language and the texts.

Later an indispensable part of processing and confirming God's call in my life came when I went to Durham, England to pursue my PhD. This was not a season of bliss or freedom from bias, but I was finally in an environment where no one, even on theological grounds, was celebrated for diminishing the contributions of women. In this time, I developed my skills as a researcher and as an advocate. With respect to the former, I found my "lane" working on interpretations of Scripture and traditions in the New Testament (especially in Hebrews, of course). During this time, I stretched out theologically; I explored whether my faith was a hindrance to careful scholarship on the New Testament, and upon deciding it wasn't, I came to a deeper understanding of how I was a theological interpreter and how I could do that in ways that honored those in the field from other traditions. I didn't abandon the convictions of my youth, but I lived them in new ways. With that, I found a holistic way to embody my commitments to peacemaking.

3. WHO HELPED YOU DISCERN YOUR CALL?

Until my junior year, no one had helped me to process my true calling. My mentors had steered me away from it. But this changed with Dr. Joseph R. Dodson, a professor at my Southern Baptist university, who answered my early questions about continuing in my education and who named my gifts when he saw them. He helped me find a seminary where my calling would not be in question (as much), and to this day he remains a dear friend and mentor. Others supported me along the way (and some certainly didn't), but Joey propelled me. He supported me in a way that made me feel that my voice was important to the church (and the academy). In this he shaped another aspect of my calling: to come alongside those battered into believing they are not gifted.

Many students have crossed the threshold to my offices over the years to process their own experiences of doubt and harm. Of all the wonderful moments that take place in the classroom, of all the writing that I have put into the world—those are the moments that I cherish the most. I could not be a professor who was faithful to my calling without replicating the generosity of Joey and others along my journey. This aspect of my call is amplified because I am a female professor. Students often know parts of my story, and they quite often make inferences about the challenges I might have faced. They wonder how to make it through when they are fighting their peers, professors, and institutions for equity. They want to know how to advocate for justice as those who lack power.

This illustrates that being a New Testament professor is far more than simply teaching courses on the New Testament. In a narrow sense, yes, my call is to illumine Scripture and to bring others to a deeper understanding of the revelation of God within these texts. But when I do this, I have audiences—my students and my readers. With my students, I have the privilege of engaging in conversations. My teaching reflects who they are more and more as I get to know them during the semester. But with my writing and my teaching, it is important to me to help my audiences process the world considering that revelation in the New Testament—to ensure that they have access to a compelling vision of God when they see leadership failures and systemic injustice.

4. WHAT GIVES YOU JOY AND WHAT'S MOST CHALLENGING IN YOUR WORK?

I love introducing students to new voices. I always assign readings with which I strongly disagree. This is not so my students can engage a straw person (i.e., an easily dismissed opponent), but so they can hear another perspective than my own, and so they can see me model charitable (I hope!) disagreement. While communicating one's disagreements precisely and humbly are among the scholars' virtues and thus were a part of my training in my doctoral program, these are skills that I hope my students replicate as they enter the world. No matter what vocation they pursue, listening and communicating graciously will serve them well in their relationships and work.

The hardest part of my calling to date is working within institutions and finding ways to serve them with integrity. Women and BIPOC often find it challenging to advocate for themselves and find a place to flourish. That has certainly been my story, and I admit that over time difficult experiences within institutions still cause me to wonder whether I "have what it takes."

5. WHAT ADVICE DO YOU WISH SOMEONE HAD GIVEN YOU ABOUT YOUR CALL/MINISTRY?

With these pains in mind, looking back, the advice I wish I had received is to ensure my call and ministry transcend my institutional ties. I recognize that many might receive this as cynicism, but it is rooted in necessary realities for the institutions themselves.

Institutions can never reciprocate a person's devotion. They are unable to by their very nature. This is because my institutions are not loyal to me alone. The decisions that institutions make could be categorized as self-interested—decisions that benefit the institution itself—or utilitarian—decisions that benefit the institution in the interest of the majority. If an institution faces a financial crisis, to save the institution (and the majority), individuals with valid callings and ministries often will be dismissed. Similarly, if addressing injustice or harm will affect the institution negatively or anger its constituents, individuals with valid callings and ministries who have been harmed often will be disregarded. This reflects the push and pull institutions receive because of market realities. Institutions reflect the broader cultural dynamics at work. Moreover, institutions are a collection of flawed human beings. Those within them may strive wholeheartedly to do what is right, but they have limited capacities and knowledge.

I think it is wise to bear this in mind as we make decisions about our callings and ministries because our callings transcend our institutional ties. When God called me to a life of studying the New Testament, he did not specify *where* that work would take place. And he could not have. I live out my calling at the educational institutions where I am employed, at the churches where my family serves, at the conferences where I deliver papers, and in the pages of my writing where I share my ideas. My calling even resides beyond where these distinct venues for my work coalesce.

This understanding that I am learning to embody allows me to do what I love—illuminating Scripture—from a place of strength and in ways that align more with my calling.

In addition to this posture, people are an important part of me keeping my call. I have a support system of other female scholars at various stages who hear me and share their own experiences. I have friends who read my work and make sure that I am continuing to grow in my research and writing in ways that honor God. Alongside this, my church family and my students help me to keep the broader relevance of my work in view.

God graciously called me to teach New Testament, and while I have scaled many hurdles, I have always had precisely what I needed to endure.

28
TEACHING OLD TESTAMENT

Carmen Joy Imes

Carmen Joy Imes is Associate Professor of Old Testament at Talbot School of Theology, Biola University. She is the author of *Bearing YHWH's Name at Sinai, Bearing God's Name, Being God's Image, Praying the Psalms with Augustine and Friends,* and *Becoming God's Family.*

1. HOW DID YOU GET INTERESTED IN YOUR FIELD/MINISTRY?

I felt a strong call to missions in elementary school that persisted into junior high and high school. As a teenager, my heart throbbed for the nations. While my classmates were at the mall, I was reading missionary biographies. While they signed up for summer camp, I signed up for mission trips. My worst nightmare was the idea of living in the United States in a house with a white picket fence. I expected to be a Bible translator working in a completely unreached area of the world.

For me, the journey into teaching came as I pursued the education I needed to become a missionary. During my first semester of college, I began to recognize that God had gifted me to teach. Looking back, it was obvious from my earliest years, but I couldn't see the forest for the trees. God opened doors for me to teach college classes even while I was an undergraduate student. Under the supervision of my professor, I found work that made my soul sing. I knew it was what I was born to do.

I still had every intention of using these teaching gifts in an overseas context as a missionary. After we got married, my husband and I pursued missions and moved to the Philippines to do Muslim outreach. I imagined that someday—after we planted a church among Muslims—we would return to the States, where I would teach missions at a Christian college. Our stint overseas only lasted two and a half years. Although we planted seeds, we came nowhere close to planting a church. I did not have the necessary experience to be a missions professor.

However, I did have an undying love for the scriptures and a desire to share that with others. I decided to pursue a master's in biblical studies. In my first semester of seminary, I realized that I needed and wanted to go "all the way." Getting a PhD would qualify me to teach at any level. I imagined I might return to my alma mater to teach the Bible. I loved the whole Bible, but to get a PhD, I had to choose between a focus on the Old or New Testament. Most churches focus heavily on the New Testament, leaving people unequipped to read the Old Testament well. Since from my perspective that was the greatest need, I chose the Old Testament.

2. HOW DID YOU PROCESS YOUR CALL?

I remember a season during which I was wrestling with whether I should pursue a degree in Christian counseling or in biblical studies. I either wanted to be a biblically grounded counselor or a Bible teacher with good people skills who could help students walk through real-life struggles. As I surveyed the field, I noticed that most counselors were female, but most Bible scholars were male. It seemed to me that the need for women's voices was greatest in biblical studies—that I could make the most difference in this field. In retrospect, I can see that academia is a better fit for me.

Returning to the United States was difficult. I felt such a strong call to overseas missions as a teenager, and I wondered if I was forsaking that call. I had dozens of growing relationships with Muslim street vendors in Manila. It was deeply disappointing to leave when we were just getting started, but for the sake of my husband's role and our mission's priorities, we decided it was wise to relocate. During that process I came to realize that God was not going to hold me accountable to a picture of my future that emerged when I was thirteen years old. God used that vision of tribal mission work to propel me forward in obedience, but I could not expect my thirteen-year-old self to have had the whole journey worked out at its first stage. The life of faith involves responding to God's leading each step of the way and remaining responsive and obedient as the needs and opportunities change. God does not promise us a whole-life vision at the outset. He asks us to trust him and take one step at a time.

3. WHO HELPED YOU DISCERN YOUR CALL?

My parents were the first to release me with their blessing, walking me to my gate at the airport (back in 1992, when that was allowed) and saying goodbye as I joined hundreds of other teenagers that they did not know to take the gospel to the ends of the earth. I was headed to Venezuela. I am so grateful for their courage to step aside so that I could respond to God's call. Later they sent me with their blessing to Bible college. When I called home to say that I thought I should become a teacher, they confirmed they had observed a teaching gift throughout my childhood. In their words, "Duh!"

Ray Lubeck was the professor who first invited me to teach Bible study methods under his supervision at the college level. When he first asked, I wondered whether it was biblically faithful for women to teach the Bible to men. When I raised that question, he took time to walk me through the relevant biblical texts, showing me how he understood them. Since I would be teaching under his authority, I came to believe it was not a violation of Scripture.

That summer after my first year of college, my home church pastor invited me to teach a class at church. I designed a six-week course on "Understanding Worldviews," which my pastor required all the elders and other ministry leaders to attend. Looking back, I'm floored at the way he shared the stage with an eighteen-year-old woman and so grateful for the opportunities he created for me to hone my skills.

During my first semester of seminary, after we returned from the Philippines, I had the sense that the academic world was where I belonged. One of my professors, Rollin Grams, pulled my husband aside and exhorted him to make sure that I pursued a PhD. He said it was a matter of stewardship and that we would not regret the decision. It was helpful to have the support of professors who knew some of what the journey ahead would entail.

Other pastors and professors along the way gave me opportunities to teach, preach, or work as their TA—helping to confirm my desire to work in higher education and serve the broader church. For many years I felt called to academia, so I could leave unanswered the question of what precisely women could do in church. More recently I have become convinced that God calls women to preach and lead alongside men, and that the church is healthier when every member contributes to the edification of the body of Christ. Over the past decade, a new phase of my calling has emerged: preaching. After years of immersing myself in the biblical text, it's a joy to bring what I have learned to equip the church.

4. WHAT GIVES YOU JOY AND WHAT'S MOST CHALLENGING IN YOUR WORK?

Teaching and writing are my twin joys. I love being in the classroom and helping students discover the riches of the Old Testament. They often come with hesitations about its relevance for the Christian life. It's a fun challenge to help them see God's grace and goodness on display in its pages. I love equipping students to have meaningful conversations about the Old Testament and to tackle difficult texts head-on. An apologist told me recently that nearly all the objections people have to the Christian faith relate to the Old Testament. My training puts me in the thick of these conversations.

For me, writing is a way to expand my classroom, maximizing the impact of discipleship on a wide range of people who may not be able to pursue formal education. Writing and speaking for the broader church makes it possible for me to fulfill my calling to the ministry. I may not be in an unreached tribal village, but I am equipping those who can go there. As I research and write, my classroom teaching is energized with new discoveries. And as I teach, I develop new illustrations that make their way into my writings.

Writing also opens doors for me to speak at churches and conferences around the world. I never dreamed that following Jesus would be so fun and fulfilling. I was ready to count the cost and go to the ends of the earth, but God has planted me in an urban jungle with a diverse cross section of students who are wrestling with so many different issues. Simultaneously, I have access to the rest of the world through travel and the wonders of the internet.

My biggest challenge is discerning which opportunities are part of the work God has called me to do and which are distractions from that calling. Sometimes I feel decision-making fatigue because so many invitations to write, speak, and teach come my way. It has helped to discover the joy of connecting other women with these opportunities. Passing on invitations to others and watching them thrive is deeply satisfying.

5. WHAT ADVICE DO YOU WISH SOMEONE HAD GIVEN YOU ABOUT YOUR CALL/MINISTRY?

Objectively speaking, if I were to plan a career in academia I should have started off with a broader liberal arts education. However, I wonder whether I would have experienced the richness of God's call to the ends of the earth in that context, and if I would have had the quality of mentoring that I received in my small Bible-college context. I am so thankful for the ways that God has opened doors for me along the way and invited me into meaningful work. I wish that someone would have told me that it is not possible to see our whole life's journey ahead of time, but that it is most important to be faithful day in and day out, trusting that God will put us where he wants us. We are not called to be successful. We are called to be faithful.

29

TEACHING PREACHING

Patricia M. Batten

Patricia M. Batten is Assistant Professor of Preaching and Associate Director of the Haddon W. Robinson Center for Preaching at Gordon-Conwell Theological Seminary. She is the author of *Parenting by Faith* and coeditor of *Models for Biblical Preaching*.

1. HOW DID YOU GET INTERESTED IN YOUR FIELD/MINISTRY?

I've always loved stories. I suppose if I gave a title to my ministry story it might sound something like this: *Not a Straight Path* or *Circuitous and Serendipitous* or *Traveling in the Slow Lane* or *The Road Less Traveled*.

From the time I was in elementary school, I envisioned myself in my dream job. I wanted to be a Sunday school teacher, like my mom. Of course, when I was seven years old, I didn't realize my mom was a *volunteer*. It seemed to me that she spent countless hours preparing weekly lessons. Surely this was her job. She was, however, never paid to teach the Bible, because it was not her job. But it was her calling. She had bins filled with construction paper and felt; scissors and glue; crayons and markers. She dogeared colorful booklets from Gospel Light and the Billy

Graham Evangelistic Association. And of course, her Bible was open and marked.

In my current role at Gordon-Conwell Theological Seminary as a part-time preaching professor, I teach men and women how to teach and preach the Bible—and make it memorable. Why do I do this? I've been changed by faithful, relevant, expository preaching. I value good expository preaching and I think our churches need to hear more of it. God's word transforms people. In a corporate worship setting, I believe God works to spiritually form the body of Christ. It's a privilege to be part of that.

2. HOW DID YOU PROCESS YOUR CALL?

My call to teach didn't mean I abandoned my call to preach. I'm a better teacher because I've been in the church preaching and I'm a better preacher because I've thought about how to teach the subject. But there did come a time when I decided that my course would veer toward the teaching of preaching. Circumstances propelled me out of parish pulpit ministry with weekly preaching and into my call to teach when I gave birth to my first child. And although I had amazing support from my champion husband and my baby-whispering parents, the weight of the church felt overwhelming while trying to learn how to nurse a baby, nap a baby, and be a nurturing mother and a loving wife. With an MDiv, ThM, and DMin in my back pocket, I knew teaching was on the horizon. In storytelling terms, our son was the inciting event that set me on a new journey into the world of academia.

Church work can be all-encompassing, and in those early years I really didn't know how *not* to think of my church at every waking moment. After many months of walking a tightrope balancing act with minimal sleep, I was eager for a call with mother's hours that didn't take up every nook and cranny of my heart, mind, soul, and strength. That call came from my former preaching professor and mentor, Scott Gibson. He was going on sabbatical, and he asked me to fill in for him.

3. WHO HELPED YOU DISCERN YOUR CALL?

In storytelling, part of the hero's journey involves an early meeting with the Mentor. The Mentor trains the apprehensive hero and gives her the tools she needs to face the challenge. The Mentor encourages and supports and has the wisdom to see that all the twists and turns of the journey, the highs and the lows, will build the character of the hero, if she is willing to learn from them. That has been Scott Gibson in my life. With his guidance, I learned the art of the lectern to teach my students the art of the pulpit.

I also learned that if you want to teach preaching, then you need to learn the art of research. After twelve years of teaching, two solo pastor parish pulpit ministries, two books, many chapters in books, a booklet, scores of speaking engagements, and three more babies, I finally commenced my PhD. Academia places priority on terminal degrees for good reason. But the academy does not always see the value that one's ministry or life experience might bring to the classroom or to research.

4. WHAT GIVES YOU JOY AND WHAT'S MOST CHALLENGING IN YOUR WORK?

Preaching is a skills course and by the end of the semester students have learned how to do something: prepare and deliver an expository sermon. There's something rewarding about participating in the journey of a preacher. Most are surprised when they learn that expository preaching is far less about diction and vocal variety and far more about understanding the biblical passage and learning to know and love one's listeners. Students learn Scripture in more depth when they teach it or preach it. Then the sermon turns around and convicts, encourages, and challenges the preacher. It's a surprising aha! moment for students when they realize that God transforms them through the act of preparing a sermon. I delight in sharing their childlike wonder in the God of the Scriptures.

Teaching is a particular joy when students spur one another on in class. The first class is filled with fear and trepidation, but as students get to know one another and realize that I want to see them succeed, then they're able to support one another, rather than compete with one another. Sometimes a class gels and forms a unique bond. I recently read that the program at Yale School of Medicine is unlike other medical schools because first-year medical students do not receive grades. This helps them form a collegial, collaborative bond. I confirmed this with a doctor who attended Yale School of Medicine, and she noted that the atmosphere was friendly and genuine bonds were formed as classmates developed supportive friendships.

Preaching isn't medical school, but faithfully handling God's word from the pulpit can make some students feel like they're in cardiac arrest. That's why I value students that value one another and lift each other up.

Sometimes it's a matter of changing one's goals from performance goals to learning goals. When students have performance goals, their main aim is to look good in front of their peers—or conversely, not to look bad in front of classmates. In the case of performance goals, a student's efforts are directed toward either being the best or not being the worst. But it's a relief to see students move toward learning goals, in which they master the art of preaching because they want to do it well and because they trust that God's word completely transforms lives.

Even when students have learning goals, unlike Yale School of Medicine I still must grade them. This is always challenging for me because students take the preaching grade very personally. They need encouragement as they enter ministry, but they also need to remember their preaching is a work in progress.

5. WHAT ADVICE DO YOU WISH SOMEONE HAD GIVEN YOU ABOUT YOUR CALL/MINISTRY?

Many of my colleagues have been men, and the overwhelming majority have been genuinely supportive. I wish someone had told them that although their path to ministry and academia is more common, their path is not the standard by which all other callings must be measured. A path that looks different has not veered off the straight and narrow, so to speak, or is not a lesser calling, or one that God will "allow" under certain circumstances. Not always, but often, a man's path to academia is straightforward: pursue a PhD in one's twenties or early thirties, gain some church experience, and then find a teaching job. My path has been more circuitous. I've been raising four kids, studying, teaching, and ministering along the way. My slower, sometimes seasonal pace of ministry and my incredibly supportive family have allowed me flexibility to engage my calling while being present with my kids. This was very important to me. I'm grateful to have chaperoned nine field trips to the farm. I think by now I could shear the sheep myself, wash the fleece, comb it out, and braid the bracelet that gets wrapped around every child's wrist. As a bonus, I picked up a few sermon illustrations along the way.

The road to becoming a full-fledged seminary preaching professor amid shrinking seminary student populations is not for the faint of heart. To begin with, you must be a consistently skillful preacher. In storytelling terms, that means the gatekeepers must give you the okay to proceed. Gatekeepers in my evangelical world have all been men, and they need to give your preaching a thumbs up. Not every sermon needs to be a home run in terms of pathos and ethos, but every sermon does need to be faithful to the biblical text. How you handle God's word is crucial.

Your preaching must also be tested in the refiner's fire of parish pulpit ministry. At least five years of pastoral experience is a must—preferably, solo or senior pastor with weekly preaching. In addition to preaching and pastoring, you must also *understand* preaching—mechanics, methods, theology, listeners—and be an effective teacher of preaching, with a thoughtful homiletics pedagogy. At the end of the day, students must be able to prepare and deliver an expository sermon, and your job is to guide them to that end.

Although important, gifting in the areas of preaching, pastoring, and teaching is not sufficient to teach homiletics to MDiv students. You also need to be active in homiletics through research and writing. Viable preaching professor candidates consistently publish in their field.

The academic road to becoming a preaching professor is studded with intimidating, rigorous, and costly postgraduate degrees. In my case, a master of divinity and a working knowledge of biblical languages are prerequisites, and a terminal degree in one's field is also necessary. I also had an opportunity to earn a one-year ThM overseas. Because I wanted to delve deeper into expository preaching with Haddon Robinson, I completed his doctor of ministry track at GCTS, which is more of a professional ministry degree. But when it comes to teaching in academia, the crown jewel is the PhD. After twelve years as an adjunct, I began to pursue my PhD in preaching and intellectual disability. It was through my research that I was introduced to a book written by Japanese theologian Kosuke Koyama, entitled *Three Mile an Hour God*. Koyama reminds his readers that walking pace is three miles per hour, the pace at which Jesus walked. It's the pace of love—a good pace, maybe even godly pace, for ministry.

My daughter, who has Down syndrome, reminds me that walking slowly gives us time to truly see people. The two of us often shuffle along the boardwalk in our city. After about a dozen paces, she sits on a curb or a bench and with her crooked pointer finger, beckons me to sit by her side. She points to leaves by her feet or a seagull squawking in the sky. She smiles and waves hello without prejudice to every single person who passes by. In the early days of our walks, I found this routine maddening because I just wanted to get to our destination. But from her perspective, there's so much to see and do along the way. Her developmental stages are drawn out in comparison to her peers, but when she does meet a milestone, we celebrate, shed some tears, and give thanks to God.

A toddler, not a terminal degree, taught me that even when I don't reach goals when the rest of my peers do, *that's okay*. I should keep working at it, hold some hands and hug some friends along the way. I can minister with a smile and a kind word right where I am. When I do reach my goals, I celebrate, shed some tears, and give thanks to God.

30
TEACHING SOCIAL WORK
Stephanie Clintonia Boddie

Stephanie Clintonia Boddie is the Fuller Family Endowed Chair for Social Justice and Associate Professor in the Diana R. Garland School of Social Work, the George W. Truett Theological Seminary, and the School of Education at Baylor University. At Baylor, she is also affiliated with the Black Church Studies program and the Environmental Humanities minor.

1. HOW DID YOU GET INTERESTED IN YOUR FIELD/MINISTRY?

With a grazed tendon and a swollen hand, I found myself at a career crossroads. I still have a scar from the accident that shifted my career from laboratory quality assurance technician to social work and later higher education. In 1991, the decision before me was to either wait for my hand to heal or take a job at the Lutheran Mission Society of Maryland (LMS) as a Compassion Center director in Havre de Grace, Maryland. This would be a new experience in many respects—a new career trajectory, a new town, a new church, a new culture, and new opportunities. My position at LMS opened the door to community service and graduate school.

Taking this job at LMS was my safe option as I delayed returning to graduate school to become a college professor. The desire
to become a college professor was sparked by my chemistry professor at Johns Hopkins University, Dr. Ruth Aranow, in 1982.
She was the only professor that seemed to care about our development as young people finding our way in such a competitive
environment. (At ninety-five, in 2025, she retired from student
advising.) My position as a foster care caseworker at Children's
Choice in Philadelphia exposed me to social work and to my first
social work professor, Louis Carter. Professor Carter was the first
African American tenured professor of social work at the University of Pennsylvania. Observing Professor Carter creatively use
his life experiences as course content to challenge his students
confirmed for me that becoming a social work professor was the
path for me. After I completed my doctorate in social welfare in
2002, my first few years as faculty at Washington University in St.
Louis were blessed with opportunities to mentor students that
are now deans, develop a community-based course working with
the St. Louis Planning Department, and consult with the Annie
E. Casey Foundation.

During the spring of 2007, I went on leave to care for my
father during his fight for life with multiple myeloma and leukemia. I lost interest in teaching social work after my father's death
in 2007. I left my tenure-track position to take a position at the
Pew Research Center. I never imagined I would return to the
academy. Eventually, I was drawn back to teaching. I taught my
first seminary classes at Pittsburgh Theological Seminary, integrating my research on congregations and my experiences as a
social worker and social work professor. This paved the path to
Baylor in 2017 and to my appointment at the Diana R. Garland
School of Social Work, the George W. Truett Theological Seminary, and the School of Education at Baylor University.

2. HOW DID YOU PROCESS YOUR CALL?

I wish I could say that from childhood my vocational call was
clear. My earliest recollection of a university professor was law

professor Charles W. Kingsfield of the movie *The Paper Chase*. I certainly never saw myself following a path into the academy. As a first-generation college student, my process for discerning my call was through *prayer, counsel, reflection, opportunities, and action.* I am grateful to have family, friends, and pastors that prayed for and with me about my vocational call. Being still in the presence of God was most helpful to gaining clarity in this process. The wise counsel of family, friends, and faith leaders helped me to see things, particularly strengths and patterns in my life that would make me successful in teaching social work. To make sense of the counsel of many people, I often reflected upon their insights by reading scripture (Isaiah 58:6–7; Micah 6:8; 1 Peter 4:10–11; 2 Timothy 1:9) and other books and taking assessments like StrengthsFinder.

Discovering that my strengths included learner and developer fit with my call to teach and affirmed that I was following the path God destined for me. Moving toward becoming a professor in a school of social work unfolded through a series of opportunities and positive experiences—my position at the Lutheran Mission Society and Children's Choice Adoption and Foster Care Services; my internships at Children's Hospital of Philadelphia and the Eastern Pennsylvania Psychiatric Institute; and serving as Dr. Ram Cnaan's teaching assistant (TA) for the courses Social Policy and Social Work in the Religious Context. Saying yes to these opportunities and my first tenure-track position at Washington University were steps outside of my comfort zone. These actions required prayer and confidence that God would supply all I needed to fulfill this vocational call.

3. WHO HELPED YOU DISCERN YOUR CALL?

My grandfather—my mother's father—was a major influence in my life. He was a deeply spiritual man that generously served his family, church, and community. I spent many weekends visiting nursing homes with him. I recalled hearing my grandfather read scriptures and share stories like the feeding of the five thousand (Mark 6:30–44). Through scriptures like this one my grandfather reminded me that God uses ordinary people, like the boy with the fish and loaves. He inspired me to resist being defined by my past and to instead find and pursue the path God set for me. He reminded me that God offers his full support to those that trust him (2 Chronicles 16:9). At my grandfather's funeral, I realized just how far he had departed from his origins on a farm in North Carolina to become an orderly at University of Maryland, a barber on the weekends, the lead deacon at a Baptist church in Baltimore, and the mentor to many. My grandfather was always there to pray and encourage me as I found my path to service from science to social work and higher education. He transitioned to heaven the year before I graduated and secured my first tenure-track faculty position. God has always placed other people on my path to help me to discern and affirm my call to teaching in social work. I have needed these fellow travelers because at the beginning of this journey I was met with lots of discouragement and opposition.

Several years before I entered graduate school, I met two strangers that challenged me to consider teaching in higher education. Both were people I met once and never met again. There were about five years between these two encounters. During these years, I felt great discontentment with my career path. These strangers entered my life and offered a perspective much different than others, particularly my parents and pastors. I did not find much support to return to college or to pursue my vocational calling to become a university professor. There was my roommate, Sandy Williams; my voice teacher, Leona Kelley Hutchins; and a college friend, Alice Kim, who was willing to meet and pray with me to discern my vocational call.

After taking the first step toward my calling, I was surrounded by leaders that supported this new direction. The McKinneys were among the first couple to open their home and their lives to me as I transitioned to serve at the LMS Compassion Center. We became family and they remained spiritual guides to help me to discern and affirm my call as doctors advised I chart a different path. Professor Carter and his wife were among those that were central in my discernment process. Fred Kauffman, my pastor during my doctoral studies, and later other pastors Stuart

McAlpine and Bo Parker expanded my vision for what God's call meant for my life. They helped me to see that I was being positioned as a university professor to serve students, the church, and the community. Being a professor is my ministry.

Help in my discernment process has often come through unexpected encounters, like crossing paths with Dr. Christson Adedoyin at a national social work conference. Dr. John DiIulio, Frederic Fox Leadership Professor of Politics, Religion, and Civil Society at the University of Pennsylvania, has played a significant role in discerning my call to teaching in social work. I have witnessed the ways he has served and equipped his students for service, created opportunities for service from Philadelphia to New Orleans to China, and used his research platform to serve the city and the nation through various positions and programs.

4. WHAT GIVES YOU JOY AND WHAT'S MOST CHALLENGING IN YOUR WORK?

My greatest joy is working with bright, gifted, and passionate students and supporting them in exploring their vocational call. Over the years, I have presented research and coauthored journal articles with students and supported them to discover their calling and complete their education, start their family, and launch successful careers. Through my Education from a Gardener's Perspective course, I have also had the opportunity to build gardens with students and to share my favorite recipes.

Still too often being the first person in certain spaces has been challenging for me. I am reminded to learn from trailblazers like Deborah, Ruth, Esther, Mary Magdelene, Lydia, Phoebe, and Priscilla. In August 2023, I received tenure at Baylor University. I am incredibly grateful that my dean acknowledged me as the first African American faculty member to receive tenure at the Diana R. Garland School of Social Work. I am also the first at Baylor to teach in three professional schools. It is a joy most days to blaze a new path by teaching at the intersection of social work, education, and theology. It can be a challenge to help others understand this work and the novel opportunities it offers for student instruction and community engagement, like my recent immersive learning course, Lamentations as Pedagogy, and the resulting film project.

5. WHAT ADVICE DO YOU WISH SOMEONE HAD GIVEN YOU ABOUT YOUR CALL/MINISTRY?

I wish someone had advised me to anticipate and plan for the challenges and crises I would face when pursuing this call and those to be faced as a professor teaching social work, especially factoring in health challenges. My car was hit by a tractor trailer during my first semester at Eastern University. This car accident triggered fifteen years of migraines, joint and back pain, insomnia, and other nagging symptoms that were first thought to be multiple sclerosis (MS) or lupus. I followed my doctor's advice and suspended my studies to focus on my health. The testimony of Christians like fellow Marylander Joni Eareckson Tada reminded me that when broken by life we can still experience the power of the Holy Spirit and serve God in ministry. I have persisted with hope knowing there will be challenges and crises ahead and God is there with me through each one.

31

TEACHING SPIRITUAL FORMATION AND ADMINISTRATIVE LEADERSHIP

Angela H. Reed

Angela H. Reed is Associate Dean for Academic Affairs, Associate Professor of Practical Theology, and Director of Spiritual Formation at George W. Truett Theological Seminary, Baylor University. She is the author of *Quest for Spiritual Community* and coauthor of *Spiritual Companioning*, and delights in serving others as a spiritual director.

1. HOW DID YOU GET INTERESTED IN YOUR FIELD/MINISTRY?

The church figures prominently in my earliest memories of wanting to know and love God. I remember well several elderly ladies of the congregation who arrived early to worship on Sundays and sat quietly in the pews. As a very small child, I asked my mother what they were doing. She told me that they came to pray. I wondered about that and many other examples of commitment to God and to a life of faith as our family showed up early and stayed late nearly every Sunday morning. My mother volunteered in education and music ministries, playing the organ for worship and funerals. My father served as a church leader and teacher in various capacities from church boards to Sunday school. The

Mennonite church of my upbringing in Manitoba, Canada, was truly a centerpiece in our lives and an essential influence in my passion for spiritual formation long before I had language for it.

I began to study the Bible for myself as a teenager. I became convinced that I should fill my mind with ideas about God through scripture, prayer, and music for as many minutes each day as I filled my mind with other content I enjoyed. I was nothing if not practical. Following the guidance of Philippians 4:7 meant making difficult choices. Some of these spiritual disciplines were taught in our church youth group and others came to me as I began to read about spiritual growth for myself. I loved to study and hoped to teach like my mother and older sister, but I could not see myself being satisfied with teaching about mathematics or language arts. I wanted to explore and understand those things that matter for eternity, and I was coming to believe that this meant the transformation of life through relationships with God and others.

In the spring of my senior year of high school, I was invited by an interim pastor in our church to provide the "meditation" for the annual church picnic. It was a pivotal moment in my calling to ministry. I was honored and filled with prayer that I might have a word of the Lord for God's people. On the day of the church picnic, it rained. Ironically, we found ourselves back in the sanctuary, and I shared my "meditation" on developing a relationship with God from behind the pulpit in front of hundreds of people who had watched me grow up. It did not occur to me then that I may have been the first woman to preach on Sunday morning. Years later, I learned that my parents shielded me from those who expressed concerns about my role that morning. I will forever be grateful for their support and that of many others who affirmed and encouraged me.

2. HOW DID YOU PROCESS YOUR CALL?

The possibility that I could become a vocational minister and even a professor was birthed in my mind in college and seminary. I began to meet and study with female professors who taught and offered leadership in various academic roles. I will never forget sitting in the office of one practical theology professor and thinking that I could not imagine a more perfect job, studying and talking with students about God and the spiritual life. I could only imagine having an office like that, filled with books and papers and students on the spiritual journey.

I processed this calling while serving in short-term mission and service assignments, and then in full-time congregational ministry. I loved the work wholeheartedly, but soon discovered that my youthful fervor could also lead to burnout. This early ministry experience taught me to slow down and turn again to the study and practice of spiritual development for myself while also tending to the spiritual health and well-being of others. I began to read Richard Foster, Dallas Willard, and many others on the nature of the spiritual life and welcomed the wisdom and guidance of family members, friends, and wise congregational leaders as I reconnected with God. These experiences only strengthened my desire to study and, ultimately, to teach other ministers about what I was living and learning.

One of the most significant influences in my calling early on was the ministry of spiritual direction. I learned about this practice for the first time while in seminary. My first spiritual director was a true mystic—a Roman Catholic educator with a deep love for God and a passion for prayer. She taught me to listen and watch carefully for potential evidence of God in daily life. I learned to listen in prayer in new ways, and I quickly discovered that this unique form of spiritual companioning was what I thought ministry was meant to be about. Spiritual direction forever transformed my understanding of growing in connection to God and living out the consequences of this relationship. I trained as a spiritual director and came to see this ministry as the heart of my calling. Today, I recognize that individual and group spiritual direction has become the lens through which I engage all tasks of ministry, including teaching and administration. It was in spiritual direction that I settled on a decision to apply for doctoral study programs, and I was shocked when the invitation came for me to study Christian education and formation at Princeton Theological Seminary. I experienced joy and peace during the visit to campus, and my husband and I discerned a calling to move our young family to Princeton, New Jersey.

3. WHO HELPED YOU DISCERN YOUR CALL?

In my twenties, family members, friends, college and seminary professors, and a spiritual director were most influential in helping me to discern a call to ministry. In my thirties, the sense of calling for academic life was shaped and clarified in doctoral studies. I arrived in Princeton after having studied at a very small school in central Canada. I was somewhat unprepared to join new colleagues who had already studied with my professors in their seminary training and knew the language and expectations of this new world. "Imposter syndrome" was strong in the early days! The support of my family and the encouragement of my new faculty mentors were essential elements for staying on the course and completing the degree.

My mind expanded weekly with every new book and class discussion. A passion for spiritual formation was encouraged in the program, and congregational studies of spiritual direction practices were supported. In fact, Richard Osmer, my primary faculty mentor, became a spiritual director himself and later wrote a book with me! I remember vividly another professor's feedback on an early assignment as I was beginning to find my way. She noted that I wrote beautifully, and then showed me how most of my academic paper needed to be rewritten. These were hard but essential lessons as I learned and grew. My professors also recommended me to faculty at George W. Truett Theological Seminary who decided to take a chance on me. I remain deeply grateful to God and to loved ones for clearing the way for me to learn and grow under the guidance of those sharing this calling who formed me in my academic work. I continue to think, teach, study, and lead with their wisdom and knowledge in mind.

4. WHAT GIVES YOU JOY AND WHAT'S MOST CHALLENGING IN YOUR WORK?

One of my great joys is the privilege of having a career that directly coincides with my sense of calling. I have had the privilege of serving as a professor and administrator, teaching and directing programs in spiritual formation at Truett Seminary over the past fourteen years. In the last three years, I have also served as the academic dean for the seminary. During that time, I have had the privilege of developing new areas of study, including a growing spiritual direction training program for seminary students, vocational ministers, and laypersons. I have also received support for the pursuit of programs and research grants in spiritual formation, spiritual direction, and disability and mental health in congregations. I would be hard-pressed to create a job description that would be a better fit for my sense of calling from God. I am humbled and grateful that God and others have entrusted me with these opportunities. This is only possible because of the generosity of those who give to a theological school and university administrators who share our vision and mission.

Ultimately, we would have no seminary if not for God's people who are drawn to prepare for ministry. I marvel every year as I hear the stories of incoming students, knowing the sacrifices they make to join us. I find much joy in the things that I am most drawn to, including spiritual care for students, teaching, and supporting faculty and staff members through administrative work. I was perfectly content with my existing responsibilities when I received the invitation to serve as an academic dean. Our dean wisely asked me to pray alongside him for someone to take on the role and, finally, I did sense the calling to this work as well. I truly enjoy praying for colleagues and students, helping them to discern what is theirs to do in God's kingdom, and building relationships beyond the seminary to the broader university and to other schools of theology.

While I love many aspects of academic work, I have found some parts especially challenging. The tenure process was demanding as I was juggling the development of several new courses, engaging in administration, conducting research, writing, and parenting young children. The support of deans who sought to release me from unnecessary tasks was essential. As I take on a growing list of administrative duties and new grant work post-tenure, I need to continue discerning what is mine to do in this season. I bring these questions to God and to my spiritual friends and guides on a regular basis. When I am heavily invested in teaching, administration, and connecting with people throughout the day, I find it challenging to engage in the kind of reading, thinking, and creating required of someone who writes academic books. Pursuing realistic goals in writing, including smaller projects, is becoming essential in a period when my days are filled with other activities.

5. WHAT ADVICE DO YOU WISH SOMEONE HAD GIVEN YOU ABOUT YOUR CALL/MINISTRY?

The most important guidance I can offer about the calling to spiritual formation in academia or in any kind of ministry is to continue to tend to one's own relationships with God and others. We cannot accompany others in their spiritual growth if we do not give sincere attention to our own life with God. If we only pray for what we need from God in ministry and for the lives of those we serve, we risk losing connection with the very purpose of our calling and with the one who gave it to us. Keeping the balance of attention to relationships with God, those God has called us to love most closely (family, friends, and church community), those we are called to serve in ministry, and our own mental, emotional, and physical well-being is a rule of life I find essential.

Finally, I wish someone had helped me to understand in my early days that perfection is not a requirement in spiritual life, in ministry, and in academia. It is possible to engage in all aspects of our shared work with excellence without aiming for a mysterious and uncertain perfection. As I consider what God truly expects of us, I grow increasingly convinced that it is joyful connection and thoughtful love and service in the world. As we take on the easy yoke of Christ, we will learn from the great Teacher who models the gentleness and humility we need for our shared calling (Matthew 11:29).

32

TEACHING THEOLOGY

Jennifer Powell McNutt

Jennifer Powell McNutt holds the Franklin S. Dyrness
Chair of Biblical and Theological Studies at Wheaton
College, where she is Professor of Theology and History
of Christianity. She is a Teaching Elder in the Presbyterian Church, an award-winning scholar, and the author of
several books, including *The Mary We Forgot* and *Know
the Theologians*.

1. HOW DID YOU GET INTERESTED
IN YOUR FIELD/MINISTRY?

It used to be that you could tell a lot about a person and their
family by entering their home and looking at the books on their
shelves. When I was growing up in the 1980s and '90s, our house
brimmed with books, from Jane Austen classics to Michael
Crichton thrillers. We had the full set of the *Encyclopedia Bri-
tannica* and the Great Books collection of the era. Copies of the
Bible, of course, abounded in our evangelical household alongside Bible dictionaries, concordances, and commentaries. John
Calvin's *Institutes* and guides to pastoral ministry were among the
treasures that lined our walls. My parents had met and married

in seminary before entering pastoral ministry together, and those books were like a cocoon as I slowly developed my wings.

In addition to the pastoral library, when you are a pastors' kid, it can become second nature to see the world through the eyes of vocational ministry. Everything, seemingly, has the potential to become a sermon illustration. From the kitchen to the couch to the car, our conversations easily gravitated toward theology in a confessional, pastoral, and practical way. In college and then seminary, I would come to understand my faith not just personally or pastorally, but historically and systematically.

I headed to college with my sights set on seminary and a traditional pulpit, but along the way, I discovered my love of the academy and theology through a historical lens. At my home church, for example, we knew of the importance of the "priesthood of all believers" taught by the Protestant Reformer Martin Luther, but I also wanted to know how Luther arrived at that concept and what was the intention of the doctrine in his time. I hoped to discover not only how theology connected to Scripture but also how the Christians of church history perceived that connection. I wanted to understand where I stood as a Christian in the Presbyterian tradition by looking back before stepping forward.

Throughout my studies, theological questions and interests developed as I matured in my reading, advanced in my academic focus, participated in educational programs abroad, and came to understand my own way of approaching topics about God, Scripture, and the church. Today, my research and writing seek to bridge theology, Scripture, and church history as my pastoral ministry aims to connect the classroom to the congregation.

2. HOW DID YOU PROCESS YOUR CALL?

At the age of ten years old, I received a clear and life-changing call to ministry while attending Fort Lone Tree Camp in New Mexico, which eventually led to my ordination as a Teaching Elder (Specialized Ministry) in the Presbyterian church. That experience at camp became a pivotal moment in my life.

As a child, I processed my call out in the open. I was too young to think to hide it and too naive to fully realize that it was controversial. So, I willingly shared it with others. As a seventh grader, I was asked by my public school algebra teacher to offer my testimony at the Fellowship of Christian Athletes one night. There, I recounted the story of my calling to ministry in the middle of a gym filled with junior high kids from across town. I knew my testimony was unusual for my age, but I felt an enthusiastic boldness and cheerfulness to share my story and conviction with others.

Along the way, I have processed my call through a life of prayer, journaling, worshiping God in a congregation, and digging deeply into Scripture. Over the years, I have benefited from the wisdom, encouragement, and support that has come from my family, childhood friends, and numerous leaders in our church. Today, I especially thrive on the partnership with my husband, David, who is also ordained. The ordination process, though long and rigorous for Presbyterians, proved useful in bringing confirmation and clarity about next steps. The opportunity to serve as a teaching assistant in seminary and my journey through the ordination process, which involved field education placement, is where I discovered my passion for the classroom.

3. WHO HELPED YOU DISCERN YOUR CALL?

I came to church history and theology through reading the work of theologians across time and traditions in their historical contexts. A milestone moment for me was when I wrote my first paper on John Calvin's *Institutes of the Christian Religion* for Professor Alister McGrath while completing a summer program at Oxford at nineteen years old. Twenty-five years later, he would write the foreword to the book that I cowrote with my husband, *Know the Theologians*. Over my educational journey, many professors—including Robert H. Gundry, James Deming, and Bruce Gordon—provided mentoring, direction, and affirmation of my gifts and abilities in ways that have made a difference in my life.

Meanwhile, it was through teaching opportunities that I began to discern my pull toward the classroom. As a ministry intern, I gained experience teaching youth, college students, and eventually adults at church. The first adult education course I ever taught was on the Reformation. When I was an MDiv student in seminary, I served as a teaching assistant for the New Testament Greek courses (I had completed a concentration in biblical languages at Westmont College). During my doctoral studies, I taught undergraduate and postgraduate students at UK universities in history, theology, and biblical studies. Each of these positions came with a chance to discover my gifts and room for growth. I was learning to weave together my training in theology, church history, and Scripture, which is reflective of my scholarship today.

Importantly, at each juncture, teaching in the academy was paired with serving in the church. Seminary is where I discerned that my call to the academy and the classroom *could* go together with a call to ordination. I grappled with this question in earnest out of the desire to be faithful to my calling and came to realize that there was precedent in my tradition and polity that would allow me to do such combined work.

It has not been a simple journey, of course. In a sense, discerning God's call is a lifelong pursuit. Opportunities come and go that must be weighed and considered through prayer and discernment. There are multiple ways that we can faithfully serve the Lord where we are and with the expertise that we have. As life unfolds and seasons change, I want to continue to be alert to how the Lord is leading me with the aid of the Holy Spirit to glorify God faithfully throughout my life.

4. WHAT GIVES YOU JOY AND WHAT'S MOST CHALLENGING IN YOUR WORK?

All the parts of my work offer opportunities for joy and bring challenges, whether in teaching, mentoring, researching, writing, publishing, or speaking. There is joy and challenge in crafting a class and thinking creatively about student formation through the material. There is joy and challenge in the pastoral care side of mentoring and supporting students as they pursue and discern their own calling. There is joy and challenge in leading worship or preparing a sermon that illumines Scripture for the congregation.

I also embrace the joy and challenge that comes with my work in serving the church.

New seasons of life and age come with adjustment as well. Unexpectedly, my first year of full-time teaching overlapped with my first year of motherhood. Our oldest daughter was born just weeks before I graduated with my PhD and began teaching at Wheaton College. The convergence of those two blessings came with tremendous joy as well as a seismic life change. That first year is a bit of a blur in my recollection, I'll admit! A few years later, a lack of maternity leave for our next child caused strain just as I was also preparing my tenure application. More recently and for the foreseeable future, the care of the family has expanded to encompass the needs of aging parents. None of this has been insurmountable, thankfully, though it has needed creative navigation and flexibility.

An added complexity of juggling motherhood and scholarship has involved sorting out the demands, expectations, and opportunities for archival research and publication, which has tended to require international travel in my field as well as conference presentations. Early on, my husband and I realized that we needed to prioritize the pursuit of these opportunities as a family so that we were never away from each other for extended periods of time. Teaching an overload, applying for research grants, and receiving the help of family in various ways has made this possible on many occasions. We carry immense gratitude for the experiences that we have shared together and the formation that it has afforded our children in terms of exposure to foreign language, history, theology, and culture. There's nothing easy about arranging those trips, but the joy that came from them has been worth the challenge required.

5. WHAT ADVICE DO YOU WISH SOMEONE HAD GIVEN YOU ABOUT YOUR CALL/MINISTRY?

I wish that I had been more prepared for how my call to ministry, which I perceived as a faithful response to God, could, in the eyes of others (even other Christians), be perceived as disruptive or unwanted. At the end of the day, there is so much that a woman in ministry and a woman in theology must navigate with care.

One of my favorite books of the Bible is the book of Acts. Those early chapters after Pentecost recount the extraordinary courage and miraculous events that took place through Peter and John's ministry of the gospel. They were aided by the Holy Spirit in conviction and boldness, and it stirred up trouble. The religious leaders regarded them as uneducated and ordinary (Acts 4:13) though Jesus himself had taught them and prepared them. Nevertheless, they were unwelcomed by the leaders of the time. They did not seem to meet the standards of the time. Gamaliel of the Sanhedrin spoke with wisdom just as the gathering was arriving at a deadly solution. With his words of caution, Gamaliel saved Peter's and John's lives by reminding the other leaders that they would not want to fight with the one who had called Peter and John.

The story encourages me in a few ways. For one, it reminds me to focus on being faithful to the call and using the gifts that God has given me, no matter the obstacles. I'm also reminded that it is not by my strength, power, or determination that my efforts bear fruit, but through the Holy Spirit and by the will of God. Finally, I am encouraged by remembering that the paths we take to our calling do not always look the same, yet the Lord still calls, equips, and sends us. Whoever we are and whatever we have, we can bring it before the Lord. I think that's an important reminder for anyone pursuing a profession in the academy and/or in ministry.

33
SERVING AS UNIVERSITY CHAPLAIN

Mary S. Hulst

Mary S. Hulst is University Pastor at Calvin University and the author of *A Little Handbook for Preachers.*

1. HOW DID YOU GET INTERESTED IN YOUR FIELD/MINISTRY?

I loved church. Loved the hymns and the Bible and the creeds and commandments. I loved the pink peppermints passed our way when the sermon began. I loved singing alto with my mom, holding the hymnal with my sister, and reading along with the sermon passage.

I loved Sunday school. Loved singing the songs and hearing from missionaries and donating pennies to buy chickens. I loved reciting my verse in Sunday school and getting a sticker on the posterboard.

I moved up from Sunday school to catechism in seventh grade. "Catechism" meant the Heidelberg Catechism, and it was taught by our pastor, Rev. Terry Lapinsky, on Wednesday afternoons. We memorized portions of the catechism while also learning its outline, authors, and the theology it taught: an explanation of the Apostles' Creed, a look at the Ten Commandments, an unpacking of each petition of the Lord's Prayer. I loved every minute.

One warm Wednesday afternoon, a few of us were talking with Rev. Lapinsky in the hallway after class. At one point, Rev. Lapinsky looked at me and said, "You're going to be a pastor when you grow up."

It was a crazy thing to say. This was the early 1980s in Holland, Michigan, in a Christian Reformed Church. Our denomination didn't ordain women. I didn't know of any women pastors. But Rev. Lapinsky planted a seed in my imagination and sparked my curiosity.

Although he left our church when I was in eighth grade, he would come back each summer to preach. As I was exiting worship, he would shake my hand and say, "Are you getting ready to go to seminary?"

2. HOW DID YOU PROCESS YOUR CALL?

I realized I had a mystery to solve. I had to figure out why our church didn't have women pastors. If I was going to take Rev. Lapinsky's words seriously, I needed to know why our church thought as it did, and then ask myself if I agreed.

My first step was to ask my high school Bible teacher. I got to class early one day. "Hey, Mr. Vanden Brink [not his real name], why don't we have any women pastors?"

"First Timothy 2," came his quick response.

I sat at my desk and opened my Bible. "But it also says not to braid our hair or wear pearls, and we do that. Why do we hold to one part and not the other?" I asked.

"Cultural context," he replied, and started the class.

Not satisfied with his answer (and, later, he wasn't either), I was curious. Why did we hold on to one part of that passage and not to the rest? I'd been steeped in scripture from my earliest days and been taught Reformed hermeneutics both implicitly and explicitly throughout my Christian day school experience. My parents had a good collection of books due to their own education in church and in the Christian school I now attended. Mom was always in a Bible study, and Dad served on denominational committees. Commentaries and copies of the Church Order were readily available.

So, I began to read.

Along the way, I found exactly one book that directly addressed the topic of women in pastoral ministry. How I found it, I do not know, and I can't for the life of me remember the title. But the book was illuminating. The author wrote about Jesus's empowerment of women, Paul's gratitude for women who were his partners in ministry, and the vision of a church in which there was no "male and female, for all of you are one in Christ" (Galatians 3:28, NRSV).

Here was someone who had gathered all that I had come to understand about the church, the Bible, Reformed hermeneutics, and the mission of God's people to clarify that not only were women allowed to be ordained, but the gospel also required it. The gospel required all hands on deck to proclaim the good news of Jesus's resurrection. The early church put women to work in all kinds of ways. The spiritual gifts laid out by Paul were never doled out according to gender. Keeping half of the church from using their gifts in leadership, teaching, or pastoral care was foolish. "We have gifts that differ" (Romans 12:6, NRSV). Let's use them!

I was energized.

3. WHO HELPED YOU DISCERN YOUR CALL?

I graduated from high school and spent six weeks of my summer in a church program called "Summer Workshop in Ministry," or SWIM. Along with three others from my area, I was sent to a church in the suburbs of Chicago to live with host families, help with VBS, hang out with the youth group, and receive intentional mentoring from the youth pastor. I loved learning about how the church functioned throughout the week. That church was also part of a different denomination that did ordain women, so there were people there who encouraged my call.

I entered college on the "pre-seminary track," a program of courses that would set me up to begin a master of divinity degree after graduation. I became good friends with the college chaplain. I remember thinking at the time, "That looks like a really fun job."

Meanwhile, our denomination was in an animated debate over the "women in office" issue. As I was moving through college, ecclesiastical bodies sorted through overtures, votes, protests, and more overtures about whether women could be elders or pastors—all adjudicated by the male elders and pastors who were allowed to attend and vote at these meetings.

I regularly ran into people who were not supportive of my call to ordained ministry. One student in my Greek class asked, "Why don't you just be a pastor's wife?" But every time someone challenged my call, within twenty-four hours someone else would affirm it: "You led chapel yesterday, right? That was good."

God kept leading me, one step at a time. This became even more clear when I was in seminary. My degree required three years of classes, one full-time summer internship after the first year, and one year-long internship for the final year. This meant that in the thick of this debate, I had to find congregations willing to have a female intern.

When the time came for me to find a summer internship, there was exactly one church willing to host me, in Colorado Springs. While the pastor and elders were glad to have me, there was a group of families who would call the church office every Friday to learn who was preaching Sunday morning. If it was my Sunday, they wouldn't come. The pastor of the church was a compassionate and kind mentor who had taken a risk to have me there and took the slings and arrows that came his way because of it. He affirmed and encouraged my call repeatedly. I remain grateful.

As I finished my classroom work and searched for a year-long internship, once again there was only one church willing to take a woman, in Iowa City. I served alongside the pastor of a small church with a ministry to faculty, staff, and students from the University of Iowa. This congregation was unanimously supportive, and their pastor became and is still a dear friend.

As graduation approached, however, I had no idea what I was going to do. The denomination had not yet opened the door for women to be ordained as pastors. I tentatively agreed to stay at the Iowa City church as an administrative assistant. It was the only church job available to me.

But much to my surprise, that June our synod recognized that while members of the denomination held two different positions on women's ordination, both could be defended from a Reformed, biblical perspective. Because of this, they said, regional church bodies could ordain women if they chose.

I could be ordained—eventually. In our denomination, ordination is a separate process from the seminary degree. You first needed to be declared a "candidate" and that would require an additional year of work—assignments that my classmates had completed during their final year of seminary.

As I was discerning my next steps, I received a phone call from a church in Grand Rapids. I had preached there a few times while I was in seminary, and they remembered me. One of their two co-pastors was leaving, and they wondered if I was willing to take a one-year interim co-pastorate while they determined their next steps. They knew I couldn't be ordained yet, but they still wanted me. I was thrilled to say yes.

I started at Eastern Avenue Christian Reformed Church in September of 1995, was declared a "candidate" in June 1996, and was ordained on September 29, 1996. I was the second woman ordained in the denomination and the first one ordained in the United States.

I absolutely loved pastoral ministry. I loved preaching, planning worship, marrying, baptizing, counseling, and moving into hard spaces with people in crisis. The congregation was growing, we were serving our neighborhood, and my professional life was thriving.

Seven years into parish ministry, I enrolled in a doctor of ministry program out of state. When I arrived at our first class, I realized I was one of only two women. The male students tolerated me but made it clear they did not agree with women as pastors. One of the teachers was not so subtle in his misogyny. The whole experience was deeply disappointing. I came back discouraged.

I met a mentor for breakfast and described my experience. "Maybe it's time for the PhD," he said. I swallowed hard. A PhD was a "someday" goal, not a "now" goal. He kept talking, laying out the benefits of timing, how a PhD was a "union card" to eventually teach, how I could apply to universities with programs in communications as well as to seminaries with programs in homiletics.

As summer went on, I thought and prayed about what he'd said. I looked up programs. I began studying for the GRE (algebra?!). I imagined how it would feel to leave these people I had come to love.

I accepted an offer from the University of Illinois. It was time to let my congregation know that I was leaving. I served eight years as their pastor, through a building project, staff turnovers, and significant losses and celebrations. It was hard to leave, but I could also feel so clearly that it was time. Stepping out of pastoral ministry was hard, but my time at Illinois brought levels of revelation and healing that ripple through my life to this day.

I defended my dissertation and applied for a tenure-track job in homiletics at Calvin Theological Seminary. I started life as a full-time academic.

And I didn't like it.

I missed being a pastor. I listened to a lot (A LOT) of sermons, but rarely preached my own. Relationships with students seemed more transactional than transformational.

In the fall of my second year as a professor, Calvin College posted the job of chaplain. Even though the job remained appealing in the years since my college graduation, I had only been at the seminary for thirteen months, and it seemed fickle to apply for something else. But one day after the job was posted, I had three colleagues email me from across the country to tell me that they had seen the posting and at once thought of me.

I applied, praying throughout that God would open this up if this was my next step and shut the door if it wasn't. God opened the door wide. I started on June 1, 2009.

4. WHAT GIVES YOU JOY AND WHAT'S MOST CHALLENGING IN YOUR WORK?

This work combines my love for the academy, the church, college students, and Jesus. I get to shepherd students as they make the faith their own. I get to come alongside my colleagues as they think about how their faith informs their work. I get to counsel our university president and serve as a confidant to members of the leadership team. I preach weekly. I pray with people. I am doing what I love.

There are some distinct differences between parish ministry and pastoring at a university. At a church, pastors engage with a wide variety of ages. I miss baptizing babies and talking with senior saints. I miss walking with people over the years.

The other significant difference is death. I never do a funeral for a dearly loved grandma who died at ninety-two. Every death on campus is a tragedy, and usually a shock. I have hard conversations about life and death and God and justice and mercy. *Why did God let this happen? How can I trust him now?* These are the deepest questions of the Christian life, and I have no easy answers. I preach the resurrection of Jesus and the hope he brings. I preach about grace. I preach about mercy. I show, I hope, how to trust in a God we don't understand.

But even in hard times, I find this work animating. I love these students. I love their energy, their playfulness, and their willingness to try new things. If a student comes to my office wondering about faith, we talk together, and I may suggest a spiritual practice or two. When we meet again two weeks later, the student will have tried the practice and have questions about it. If I suggest they go to our counseling center, they go. If I offer to read a book with them, they'll do it. Because of their stage of life, they are curious and teachable. Every spring I watch students walk across the stage and delight in how much they've grown.

5. WHAT ADVICE DO YOU WISH SOMEONE HAD GIVEN YOU ABOUT YOUR CALL/MINISTRY?

When I speak with students who are anxious about their futures, wondering about jobs or internships or graduate school, I remind them that they only need one door to open, just one. They don't need four job offers, or six grad school options. They need one.

At each juncture, God opened the next door exactly when I needed it. Just one. One summer placement. One church internship. A one-year interim co-pastorate that became an eight-year joy. And through it all, God never let me wallow in discouragement. He provided the daily bread of affirmation just when I needed it.

As Paul writes in 1 Thessalonians 5:24 (NRSV), "The one who calls you is faithful, and he will do this." He did, and he does. I am so grateful. Great is his faithfulness.

CONCLUSION
Patricia M. Batten

Patricia M. Batten is Assistant Professor of Preaching and Associate Director of the Haddon W. Robinson Center for Preaching at Gordon-Conwell Theological Seminary. She is the author of *Parenting by Faith* and coeditor of *Models for Biblical Preaching*.

REALITY CHECK/ENLIGHTENMENT

This book drips with authenticity. We haven't candy-coated our calls and the challenges we've faced pursuing them. We wrote with a genuine desire to share the real joys and struggles of following Christ as the "fairer" sex so that you will be informed and perhaps leave with some small nugget of wisdom that might help you in the future and know that you're not the only woman walking in this strange women-doing-ministry world. You're not alone. We've been there.

Too many times throughout my ministry, I was left tongue-tied because someone said something to me that knocked me off-balance. I've struggled to know when to challenge, when to ignore, when to reply with wit or humor, or when to follow up later with a "You know, when you said. . . ." Over the years, on multiple occasions, both men and women who held more tightly to complementarian views than they did to love and kindness have walked out of the sanctuary when I stood to preach. Some have told me that when I'm on the schedule, they refuse to enter the sanctuary or even come to church. One elder asked to meet me two days before I preached at his church under the guise of "getting to know me better" since he would be introducing me on Sunday. Instead, he grilled me for an hour about my preaching passage even though I had been invited to preach by the pastor and elder board. I felt more like a suspect in an interrogation than a welcomed guest. He also gave my sermon a disapproving post-mortem via email.

Some comments hurt, while others are more humorous. My first church was built in the 1830s and followed a color scheme common among Baptist churches in the area: pink interior walls and red carpeting in the sanctuary. A visitor bounded into the sanctuary one Sunday morning and announced, "I knew it had to be a woman preacher. She painted the walls pink!" For the record, my favorite color is *blue*.

My default response to critical or even wacky comments has been a lips-sealed smile, brows raised, slight head cock, and a disbelieving nod, culminating in a single vocal slide high-to-low "Ohhhhh." That's because so many of these comments that come from Christians confuse me by their blatant disregard for love. The work is hard enough without someone challenging you or criticizing you at every turn and making you feel like you shouldn't be in the position you're in. *Even though you're good at it. And God called you to it.*

The reality check is that as a woman you often have an extra layer of complicating factors. Many of these complicating factors are not inherently bad, but onlookers perceive them as strange. Raising a family is complicated for pastor moms and female leaders in ministry. A first gentleman or a female pastor's husband confuses some people. Single female pastors or single female Christian leaders are sometimes objects of suspicion. Anything that's outside of the norm tends to frighten people. As a pastor's spouse, my husband has accrued his own stories and often asks when he can write a book from his perspective. In my first pastorate (with the pink interior), he was taken into the church basement, which was only accessed through an outside makeshift plywood panel. A rickety set of stairs led to an even ricketier lawn mower. There, in the dim light of the basement, he was ordained mower of the church lawn. My husband remarked that if *I* had been the ministry spouse, I never would have been asked (or told) to mow the lawn. Touché.

ENCOURAGEMENT

You, reader, have your own story and your own call. Consider writing it out. Answer the questions we wrestled with in this book. Scribble them down in a notebook. Type them out on your laptop with a latte by your side. Pay attention to your own feelings as you mull over answers. What is your tone? Are you filled with hope? Or are the challenges of following Christ vocationally turning you sour? What questions are you still working out? *Pray over them.* How would you describe your call? What people come to mind when you think about your call to ministry? What advice would you give to a younger woman who is considering her call? What questions still linger after reading this book? Use this book to begin to come to terms with God's calling on your life. Whose story most resonated with you? Where do you go from here?

WHAT'S AT STAKE

Here's what's at stake: a church and a world that function contrary to God's intention because you are not present or your call to use your gift has been unwelcome. The apostle Paul uses the imagery of a body to describe the usefulness and necessity of every single person in the body of Christ. He's talking about the unity of the body of Christ through diversity. Unity does not equal homogeneity. Instead, God desires to achieve unity in the body of Christ through diversity.

> If the whole body were an eye, where would the sense of hearing be? If the whole body were an ear, where would the sense of smell be? But in fact God has placed the parts in the body, every one

of them, just as he wanted them to be. If they were all one part, where would the body be? As it is, there are many parts, but one body. (1 Corinthians 12:17–20, NIV)

Ignoring the call you have from the Lord presents an incomplete witness to the world and a lopsided way of doing ministry in the church. When you are not using your gifts in the church, in academia, in parachurch ministries, and at home, then those structures are incomplete. They lack the diversity you can bring them—for the sake of unity. You are uniquely qualified to reach people in a way that someone else is not.

WHAT IT COULD BE

We have talked about what is at stake when women *do not* pursue their calls from God to follow Christ vocationally. But let's face it: Fear is often a poor motivator. In addition to talking about what is at stake, it's crucial to paint a picture of what the church and our world might look like when women *do* follow Christ and are welcome to do so. In order to do that, I need to tell you about Jean.

Jean was a single mother in the 1990s who attended a congregational church that had been established in 1698. More than a few members were entrenched in their New England ways of doing church. But as a single mom of three, Jean saw a need in her community that others might have overlooked. The region lacked childcare. Jean prayed about it and spoke to her pastor. Why couldn't their church build a daycare—a Christian daycare to meet the needs of young families in their community?

Jean managed the project—not the building of a physical structure, but the building of a daycare, one that demonstrated the love of Christ to every infant, toddler, and parent who walked through the doors. She had to build a staff, write a handbook, immerse herself in state safety regulations and requirements, acquire equipment for the playground, and gather changing tables, cribs, and toys, among a million other details. Jean reached out to her community. She advertised. She prayed. *A lot.* There were times when Jean wondered if it would come together, but her pastor continually encouraged her. That made all the difference.

Thirty years after the doors to the daycare opened, I became the pastor of the church. Jean is now in her eighties and her daughter oversees the daycare. One Sunday, a young woman sat alone in a pew. She had come a handful of times before, but I hadn't gotten the chance to connect with her. I had just finished preaching on Jeremiah 29:11: "For I know the plans I have for you. Plans to prosper you and not to harm you" (NIV). I explained how God had good plans for the Israelites—plans to bring them home—even though they had walked away from God and were in exile. If they would just seek God with all their hearts, then God would bring them home. After the service was over, I greeted the young woman. "What brought you here today?" I asked. She said, "I haven't been to worship in a while, but this church is home to me. It's always been home. I came to the daycare as a baby."

Jean built a daycare that poured a foundation of faith for scores and scores of children and parents. Her pastor fully supported her. Because Jean followed God's call, that young woman sitting in the pew, and countless others, learned how to seek God and answer his call to come home to him.

FULLY PARTICIPATING IN GOD'S WORK

We have labored to demonstrate that the work of women in the church, the academy, and in a variety of ministry venues *is the work of God*. The apostle Paul says in Ephesians 2:10: "For we are God's workmanship, created in Christ Jesus to do good works, which God prepared in advance for us to do" (NIV). It's the building of the kingdom (sometimes through a daycare) by the hands of creative, constructive women. It's the shaping of a new generation to form a heart and mind for Christ. It's the time spent investing in people who feel overlooked and unloved in this world. It's boosting those who lack confidence and pouring courage into the discouraged. It's correcting in love and pursuing God-given dreams while pressing past challenging obstacles. It's navigating relationships; navigating expectations; navigating failure; navigating criticism.

We hope we've shed light on some of the challenges and some of the joys and delights experienced by women who follow God's call. Few, if any, sailed into their calling on smooth seas. Some have been cut on the sharp corner of criticism, while others are still catching their breath from the rough seas of regret. Still, many women rise like the swell of an ocean wave, until they finally break prejudices and stereotypes, reaching and watering a dry and weary land.

AFTERWORD

Nijay K. Gupta

Nijay K. Gupta serves as Julius R. Mantey Professor of New Testament at Northern Seminary and is the author of the award-winning book *Tell Her Story: How Women Led, Taught, and Ministered in the Early Church.*

As I read through the reflections, stories, and practical wisdom of the faithful women who contributed to this book, it felt like a sacred honor to read their words. Behind these essays are real lives, and I know those lives have included blood, sweat, and many tears. That doesn't take away from the joys and high points of ministry these women have experienced. But a common thread in several essays (and a subtext in several others) is *you are not alone.* If you are a woman pursuing your calling in ministry, this is a crucial reminder, because there are always going to be voices out there telling you that you don't belong. So, seek out those mentors and groups where you can feel affirmed in your calling and where you can lean on other women.

But as I continued to reflect on the importance of finding support and affirmation from others, I couldn't help but turn to scripture (occupational hazard of mine), specifically Luke 1:39–56, which includes Mary's Song of Praise (also known as "The Magnificat"):

[39] A few days later Mary hurried to the hill country of Judea, to the town [40] where Zechariah lived. She entered the house and greeted Elizabeth. [41] At the sound of Mary's greeting, Elizabeth's child leaped within her, and Elizabeth was filled with the Holy Spirit. [42] Elizabeth gave a glad cry and exclaimed to Mary, "God has blessed you above all women, and your child is blessed. [43] Why am I so honored that the mother of my Lord should visit me? [44] When I heard your greeting, the baby in my womb jumped for joy. [45] You are blessed because you believed that the Lord would do what he said."

[46] Mary responded,

"Oh, how my soul praises the Lord.
    [47] How my spirit rejoices in God my Savior!
[48] For he took notice of his lowly servant girl,
    and from now on all generations will call me blessed.
[49] For the Mighty One is holy,
    and he has done great things for me.
[50] He shows mercy from generation to generation
    to all who fear him.
[51] His mighty arm has done tremendous things!
    He has scattered the proud and haughty ones.
[52] He has brought down princes from their thrones
    and exalted the humble.
[53] He has filled the hungry with good things
    and sent the rich away with empty hands.
[54] He has helped his servant Israel
    and remembered to be merciful.
[55] For he made this promise to our ancestors,
    to Abraham and his children forever."

[56] Mary stayed with Elizabeth about three months and then went back to her own home. (NLT)

Mary of Nazareth was not an ordained pastor or seminary professor or overseas missionary in a formal sense. But I am struck by how much Mary's story parallels that of many of the women in this book. So perhaps you can find some comfort and encouragement in her struggles, faith, and endurance. Here are some things I noticed, and I hope this is a text you will turn back to for inspiration and encouragement from time to time.

In the passage just before the Magnificat, we read about the Annunciation (Luke 1:26–38), where Mary is visited by the angel Gabriel. He tells her that she is special to God and God will use her in powerful ways to bring about the kingdom. While she is rightfully perplexed and confused, her hesitation gives way to faith and acceptance: "I am the Lord's servant. May everything you have said about me come true" (Luke 1:38, NLT). You may not have an angel visit you and pronounce prophecy, but there will often be "holy moments" where your calling is made clear, whether in a special experience (at a camp or retreat), or in quiet prayer, or through the words of a friend or mentor. Hold onto those moments, write them down, return to them for encouragement.

The first thing (according to Luke) Mary did after the angel left her was plan a trip to see her cousin Elizabeth. You don't need to be a genius to know why. She wanted to share her experience with someone who would understand. They could celebrate the Lord's grace together, and no doubt they could support each other in the inevitable pains of pregnancy. We learn that she stayed *three months*. That's a long visit! Sometimes you just need a quick coffee and chat with a mentor. Sometimes you need a weekend. And sometimes you need a few months! Find those confidants who will invest in you deeply and journey with you for the long haul.

In the first part of Mary's song, she recognizes the gift of serving God. God has richly blessed her with the opportunity to contribute to the work of the gospel (1:46–49). In one's calling, especially in the church, there will be critics and skeptics, and it is easy to lose sight of the joy of participating in the redemptive work of God. Mary's song shifts from God's blessings on *her* ("he took notice of [me]" in 1:48) to the pattern of God's blessings throughout time for all of God's people ("he has helped his servant Israel" in 1:54). This is a reminder to take the *long* view. God has used women to further his redemptive plan many times throughout history, including figures like Deborah, Ruth, and Hannah. Your story is part of a big story of good news that God is telling.

Mary knew what it was like to be on the margins. She referred to herself as a "lowly servant girl" (1:48). She also knew that many would look at her with suspicion when they found out she was pregnant. There would be rumors that she was unfaithful to Joseph, and some would doubt her story about a divine visitation. But it is no coincidence that her song prophesies the overturning of world systems, whereby the arrogant will be humbled, corrupt leaders will be deposed (1:51–52), and God will do right by those who have been deprived (1:53). The bottom line for Mary is *there is always hope when God is in the mix.* Mary knew hard times would come for her, and she professed the truth that God is in the business of turning things upside down to right the wrongs of the world. If you are a woman following Christ in your calling, I encourage you to return to these words if you encounter times of setbacks. God's not done yet; the story isn't over.

Mary's song comes at the beginning of her story after her calling. So, what do we learn from the rest of her life? It can be boiled down to this: *She showed up for Jesus.* She nudged him to help at the wedding in Cana. She checked up on him during his ministry years. She even showed up at the cross and saw the painful death of her beloved son. And then *after* that, she showed up in the upper room in Jerusalem when the Spirit came down at Pentecost (Acts 1:14). She was faithful in her calling from beginning to end; often that means showing up for Jesus when you want to—and even and especially when you don't. It's easy to show up for a party in Cana; it's not easy to show up on a dark day in Golgotha. But Mary was there. Embracing your calling is not a one-off choice. It is a daily, even hourly, decision to trust and obey.

I encourage you to have texts like this that will inspire you and encourage you throughout your ministry. Mary has long been recognized as a model of Christian discipleship: thoughtful and curious, responsive to God, jubilant in worship, resilient in faith, and obedient until the end. There is only one Mother of God, but there are countless "Marys" following Christ then and now. Go and be a Mary, too.

A FINAL WORD

Tara Beth Leach

Tara Beth Leach is senior pastor of Good Shepherd Church in Naperville, IL. She is the author of several bestselling books, including *Emboldened* and *Radiant Church* and a cohost of The Pastors Table Podcast.

There is a conundrum that many women find themselves in when the topic of women in ministry comes up—a topic that's been hashed and rehashed, debated and dissected, often to the point of exhaustion. But here's the thing: most of us don't step into ministry to talk about women in ministry. We don't feel the Holy Spirit's stirring in our souls, driving us to preach, teach, shepherd, and lead, just so that we can defend the calling on our lives.

No, we go into ministry because Jesus has captured our hearts. We're compelled to tell the world about the Savior who has turned our lives upside down with his love. We step into this calling because we long to see every knee bow and every tongue confess that Jesus Christ is Lord (Philippians 2:10–11). We go into ministry because the vision of the Bride of Christ—radiant, pure, and reflecting the glory of God—burns within us. We're emboldened by the Spirit to preach the gospel, to shepherd God's people, to lead them into the fullness of life in Christ. We step into this calling because we simply cannot imagine doing anything else.

But then, there it is—the conundrum. We step into the pulpit, ready to proclaim the good news, and we're met with silence or, worse, skepticism. We lead, but our leadership is questioned, not because of our character or competence, but because of the shape of our bodies. We prophesy, but our words are dismissed as emotional or overzealous. We care for the local church, pouring out our lives in service, yet our efforts are sidelined because we are women.

And this is where the awkwardness settles in. Because for many of us, we've been taught not to fight for ourselves. We've been raised to be caregivers, to put others first, to stay quiet and submissive. But maybe, just maybe, the work of the church is to reframe this conversation. Maybe we need to shift our focus from fighting for a seat at the table to something far more important—being faithful to the call of God on our lives.

This isn't just a conundrum; it's a clarion call for the church. The conversation about women in ministry isn't just an issue to be debated; it's a reminder of who we are as the people of God. When we go back to scripture, we see the Great Commission in Matthew 28:18–20. Jesus didn't limit this commission to men; he sent all his disciples to make more disciples, to baptize them, to teach them everything he commanded. The Great Commandment in Mark 12:29–31 calls each of us to love God and love our neighbor. And in Acts 1:8, the sending mandate commissions us to be his witnesses, to the ends of the earth. These aren't gendered instructions; they're invitations to every believer.

The apostle Paul, often cited in these debates, provides a framework in 1 Corinthians 12 that's all about the diversity of the body of Christ. Different gifts, different roles, but one Spirit, one body, not gender exclusivity. Instead, Paul emphasizes that what matters is our life in the Spirit, our obedience to Jesus, and our love for God and neighbor.

Yet, here we are, still grappling with this conundrum. Not because the biblical mandates are unclear, but because our cultural lenses have clouded our vision. For far too long, interpretations of scripture have been shaped by cultural norms rather than the radical inclusivity of the gospel. This isn't about fighting for our place—it's about being true to the mission of God. It's about living into the fullness of what it means to be the body of Christ, where every part, every gift, every voice is essential.

Too often, women in ministry are treated as exceptions, as anomalies that need to be explained or justified. We're asked to defend our calling in ways that our male counterparts rarely, if ever, must do. But we carry this burden because we know—deep in our bones—that our call comes from God.

The conversation around women in ministry can sometimes feel like a debate, but it doesn't have to be. Instead, it can be an opportunity for the church to grow, to expand its understanding of what it means to be the body of Christ. It's a chance to embrace the diversity of gifts that God has given his people and to see how, together, we can reflect the fullness of his love and grace.

But here's the truth: The church needs women in ministry. Our voices, our perspectives, our gifts—they're not just nice to have; they're essential to the health and growth of the body of Christ. The mission of God requires women and men, young and old, to walk in the power of the Spirit. Just as the body has many parts, the church is enriched by the diverse voices and experiences of all its members. We bring something unique, something vital, and the church is brighter—more radiant—when women live into their complete calling in Christ, propelled by the Holy Spirit.

I imagine a church without this conundrum. A church where female senior pastors are not an anomaly. I imagine the church Peter imagined—one where sons *and* daughters prophesy (Joel 2:28; Acts 2:17). I imagine a church where women simply get to pastor because that is what they were called to do.

The conversation about women in ministry isn't just about gender; it's about faithfulness to the gospel. It's about ensuring that the church is fully equipped to carry out its mission in the world. It's about living into the reality of the kingdom of God, where there is neither Jew nor Greek, slave nor free, male nor female, but all are one in Christ Jesus (Galatians 3:28).

And in the end, the question isn't whether women should be in ministry—it's how we can be faithful to the mission of God by embracing the gifts and callings of all his people. It's a call to unity, to mutual respect, and to the full participation of every believer in the work of the kingdom. And it's a call that we must answer together, as the body of Christ, with courage, with love, and with a commitment to the radical, life-changing gospel of Jesus Christ.

www.ingramcontent.com/pod-product-compliance
Lightning Source LLC
Chambersburg PA
CBHW020531191025
34214CB00001B/1